After Life, After You

True Stories of Love, Grief and Hope

S.K. REID

JCP

First published by Jane Curry Publishing 2010
(Wentworth Concepts Pty Ltd)
PO Box 780 Edgecliff NSW 2027

Web: www.janecurrypublishing.com.au

National Library of Australia
cataloguing-in-publication data:
    Reid, S. K.
    After life, after you : stories of life, love and hope.
    ISBN 9780980721263
    Bereavement. Loss (Psychology)
    155.937

Design: Cheryl Collins Design
Printed in Australia by McPherson's Printing Group

In loving memory of Stu

Contents

Preface

Perhaps more than any other human experience, the death of a partner evokes powerful, unfamiliar agonies of the body, heart and soul. The death of a partner transports us into an unfamiliar emotional landscape where we need to find a new identity, purpose and way of living.

This landscape of grief causes us to re-evaluate ourselves and our relationships. If we don't have other strong emotional relationships, then we may find the experience unbearably isolating, disorienting and bewildering. Even when death is expected through age or illness, it comes as a mighty shock. There seems to be no viable preparation no matter how much it is expected.

The consciousness that enlivens each one of us does not stop at the perimeter of our physical body. Indeed our body exists within our consciousness rather than our body having a consciousness. The electro-magnetic energy of the heart can be measured two or three metres away from the body. This field goes much further but we lack the instrumentation to measure its subtlety. Psychologists sometimes refer to this as our 'body map'. Amongst other things, it provides us with spatial awareness. For example, when you drive a car your consciousness expands to encompass the whole of the vehicle which makes manoeuvring it possible. Even though it is out of sight, we know within a couple of centimetres how close our bumper is to the car in front when parking the vehicle.

When we embark upon a journey into an unknown landscape we generally take a map which shows us the various interconnections of highways and byways. Likewise, our body map represents all aspects of our bodily self, inside and out. Together these invisible maps create our physical and emotional awareness and provide us with a sense of who we are in both physical and emotional relationships. These body maps can be profoundly elastic and extend and contract according to the clothes we wear, the car we drive, the house we live in, the people we love and the social environments in which we move.

This happens most powerfully through our relationships, so it is little wonder that when our partner dies we are confronted with a re-evaluation of who we are, what our purpose is and, for some, whether life is worth living. The pain and disorientation of bereavement may well evoke feelings of helplessness, isolation and sap the will to live.

We have lost the solid ground of our relationship and we feel disoriented, confused, shocked and sick in the stomach from the sheer unfamiliarity of our emotional landscape.

When we love someone our consciousness becomes enmeshed in that of our beloved. We become as one and this allows us to know what our partner is thinking or feeling. Love - even at great distance - knows no bounds.

The love that binds us together gives us a sense of who we are in relation to our environment, our sense of place and meaning in our lives. We don't lose our sense of 'self' but acquire another and larger 'self' that encompasses us both. The death of a partner rips open the fabric of our shared consciousness and we no longer know who we are, we lose our sense of place and all meaning can slip through the cracks of our broken heart.

There is no timeframe for grief as there is no timeframe for love. Some people will move through the profound changes with relative ease while others will struggle to find a meaning for their life and any reason to exist given that the foundations of their life, literally their map for life, has been so shaken or destroyed.

The opposite of death is birth, not life. Life, consciousness, love, is indestructible, invisible, all pervading and the essence of our being. Love never dies. It is our ability to connect to the essence of our being that enables us to let go of the physical form of our bodies or to perceive that our loved-ones are no less alive now that they have physically departed from us.

In this lies the great mystery of life and love.

Every person's grief is personal and unique. The people within this book have provided us with an insight into the vagaries of living, loving and loss when a partner dies.

Petrea King
Author of *Sometimes Hearts Have to Break*, (Random House)
Founder of The Quest for Life Foundation
www.questforlife.com.au

Introduction

Into The Blue

In August 2002, my husband passed away in his sleep. His death was sudden, and unexpected. Stu was only thirty-three years old. His death completely shattered my world. This book has been written in response to my experience of his death, and the incredible isolation and agonising grief in which Stu's death left me.

A telephone call bore the news. It was the most dire moment of my life.

To see his stone cold, lifeless body lying in a casket was one of the most harrowing and shocking experiences I have ever had. The gentle, warm hands which once held me, were now cold and neatly crossed over his chest; the beautiful, deep, brown eyes which once looked into mine, were now forever closed; the full lips that had passionately kissed my own, were now pale and drawn; the beautiful, handsome man that had been my soul mate, my best friend, my lover, was now a corpse; his lifeless body lying before me, cold, still, and dead.

I had witnessed death before, and had lost people close to me, but nothing prepared me for this. The brutal reality of it struck me in a way that I had never experienced. The totality, the finality, the absoluteness of death was something that I struggled to come to grips with. Even now, I seem to lack the compartment in my head that will comprehend what death is. Instead, it seems to be an unknowable concept that brings with it associated thoughts, perceptions and experiences.

Encountering death is a life-altering experience, and one that leaves those in its wake forever changed. This book explores this shift and change.

One of the many painful things about losing Stu was how it changed my sense of reality. I became a sadder, less confidant, more depressed person. Over time, I have had to consciously and deliberately re-cultivate the skills required to participate in everyday life. I have had to learn how to be strong and brave, to be capable of laughter, and to be able to find joy once again.

Yet every one of these new skills is tempered by the ever-present shadow of death and the sadness that it brings. As such, what emerges is a new way to experience and interact with the world. I liken this in many ways to being born again: when a loved one dies, we are forced brutally into a new way of being, into a new and unfamiliar experiential world.

In my own case, this new and unfamiliar world presented me with many emotional challenges, two of which stand out.

Firstly, I found there to be no road maps or guidebooks for dealing with death and its aftermath. I was in a completely unfamiliar landscape: there was unbearable pain and a relentless march of time pushing my beloved Stu further and further away from me; there was a stark contrast between my tormented inner world and the insane normalcy of everyday life. I was possessed by an overwhelming desire and all consuming need to wind back time, to wake up from this nightmare. I was gripped by a deep physical need; an unbearable longing and gut wrenching ache to just see him, to be with him again. The world about me became flat and colourless where once there had been warmth and light. The vibrancy of his life had vanished, leaving a dull monochromatic veneer across everyday life. Everywhere I turned I was reminded of Stu's absence, and all I wanted to do was to scream and yell and rage and to shake him into being, but he was absolutely nowhere to be found.

This place was hell on earth. It was frightening, intensely alienating, emotionally and mentally confusing. For a while, I could not bear to live without him. For a time, my pain was so overwhelming, so intense, that I found it extremely difficult to go on living. Somehow, I managed to find a reason to stay, to keep on hanging on. And the gift that waited for me, that made hanging on worthwhile, was the knowledge that my being here mattered, that in spite of whatever anguish I may have felt, that the gift of life in itself is reason enough to be here. From my own experience of the death of someone close to me, have came lessons worth sharing with others.

One of these has been about death itself.

For an experience that is so universal in its relevance

to human life, why then is death so shrouded in secrecy and silence?

I suspect it has much to do with the way our Western lifestyle and attitudes favour the avoidance of unpleasant things. Yet in sweeping unpleasant things under the carpet, we are robbed of the opportunity to cultivate the skills required to be better emotionally equipped to cope with such things. Moreover, the absence of dialogue about death in the broader context of how we live our lives results in a tendency to take our lives for granted.

It is not until we lose someone close to us that we fully appreciate how overwhelmingly precious life is, and how little time we truly have to enjoy the blessing of existence itself.

If we collectively and individually lived our lives with a greater appreciation of this truth, then our lives would be far richer for it.

Surely atrocities such as war and the savage treatment of our fellow humans make little sense when we truly value the gift of life?

The anguish of personal pain that comes with such a loss allows us to relate to the universality of human suffering. When a loved one dies, all at once we understand the torment of a mother in Iraq whose child has been an unwitting casualty in a war fuelled by fear, hatred and misunderstanding; or the wife of the policeman who didn't make it home on the day the towers collapsed; or the orphan who lost an entire family in the killer waves of the Tsunami; or the parents who lost their only children to the ravages of one of the world's worst bushfires ever. The anguish of personal pain reminds us that life can indeed be short.

When Stu died, I was struck with a shock that was toxic to my sensibilities and awareness. I couldn't understand how the world kept going as if nothing had happened. After seeing his cold, lifeless body in that casket, I could not comprehend how people were going about their daily lives completely oblivious to the privilege of this precious gift of life that they embodied. It seemed obscene to me that they were not celebrating the miracle of their skin being soft and warm to the touch because this amazing thing called blood flowed freely through their veins, bringing oxygen and life to their bodies; that because they were alive and their hearts were beating, they could move their legs and walk around; that they could fill their lungs with cool, wintry air and breathe; that their moist, bright, living eyes would be blessed with the sight of the setting sun or the rise of the full moon; that their ears could hear the symphony of birdsong greeting the breaking dawn; and that their being could behold the very certainty that the sun would rise once again to bring them a whole new day on which to etch their story.

It was some time before the intensity of this shock softened. It became evident to me that most people are spared this brutal lesson for much of their lives. For many people, it may not be until they are much older, when death is perhaps more expected, that they will endure such lessons. For those of us who learn about the pain brought by death earlier, we find a more challenging path awaits us.

The other thing that troubled me greatly after Stu died was how people, other than close family, behaved towards me.

As is often the case with traumatic events in our lives, friends and acquaintances become polarised into two distinct camps -- those who sincerely care for one's welfare, and those who don't. It is said that in times like this, you 'learn who your friends are'. Very quickly, it became apparent which friendships were based on substance and which were built from flimsier material.

There were times when I desperately needed the shoulder of a friend to lean on and shoulders were more often than not, in very short supply.

I remember one time in particular when I emailed two friends about my upcoming wedding anniversary, telling them how difficult a time this was for me. I waited for, but received no reply. Again I emailed, as the day drew nearer. Again, no reply. I emailed one final time, and told them that I could have done with some emotional support on this day, and that I was off to the cemetery to 'celebrate' my wedding anniversary with my two dogs. Then, just as I was about to leave for the cemetery, I received two emails from the two friends concerned. "At last!" I thought. "Finally they reply to my emails!" I eagerly opened the first and then the second email. To my utter disbelief, they were both general emails, one regarding the damage from the unseasonable February storms of the day before, the other a sickly sweet chain mail about supporting friends in need! I was shocked and deeply hurt. Neither friend had bothered to acknowledge my emotional state at that time, let alone reply to the emails I had sent.

Sadly, this was to become a familiar theme in my life, and only has really ceased since I stopped seeking from others the comfort I so desperately sought. Friends seldom checked in to see how I was travelling, to see how I was coping. Anniversaries, birthdays, Christmases all were times of heightened emotional sensitivity, occasions when one feels most alone, and yet these were the times when the silence from others was at its loudest.

Again, I see this having a lot to do with Western society's aversion to things unpleasant, particularly death. Moreover, it seems that many people simply do not know how to deal with death and emotional trauma. We are bombarded nightly in our lounge rooms with images and stories on television of death and tragedy that desensitise people to some extent about the suffering of others. Perhaps people feel too threatened by suffering, fearing it may upset the illusion of security upon which their daily lives are precariously balanced.

With a view to engendering a more compassionate and gracious way to respond to one another in times of need, it is hoped that this book will be of some value to those who seek greater understanding of what their friend, son, daughter, brother, sister, mother or father may be experiencing in their bereavement.

The Other

I have focused my exploration of the impact of death on the loss of the significant other; the spouse or partner. As human beings, our identity is informed by our history, biology and biography, and our relationship with our partner is a unique relationship that is particularly influential on whom we are as individuals.

Our identity is also shaped by the evolution of self that takes place within a relationship. Each relationship with another human being is unique. The way we are with one person will be different to how we are with somebody else. The 'signature' of that relationship, the prevailing dynamic governing the connection and ongoing dialectic, is contained both within the space that is created between the two people, as well as the space occupied by each. It is in relation to our partner, our significant other, that the shape of our selves gains definition.

In the company of our partner, the passage of time is marked, and our personal history carved from shared experience. The dreams, hopes, goals, ambitions, successes, failures, expectations and disappointments of two people are shared, tested and challenged, and behavioural patterns between the two emerge and remain deeply held. It is alongside and in relation to our partner that identities are forged, that the outside world is navigated, and that meaning is defined and reality co-created. Most of all, it is with our partner that our deepest, most personal intimacies are shared.

When he or she dies, one half of a union made up of two individuals is shattered. The surviving individual is left as sole custodian of the shared memories of a life that was built around an intertwining of two lives. The dialectic disappears. Where once two people could reminisce about places they had been, and things they had done together, all of a sudden there is no-one to offer a response within what has been up until that moment a two-person dialogue. There is only monologue, and memories that were shared become reminders of what has been lost.

There is an agonising emptiness and unbearable isolation in this, and it can be a brutally, disturbingly lonely experience in and of itself.

With the death of the significant other, an entire world just disappears. We catch ourselves in a flashback, suddenly remembering something or perhaps finding ourselves in a place frequented in the past by 'two of us'.

Just the other day, I drove past a building where I had done a film shoot many years ago and which I hadn't seen since that time. The immediate impulse was to share this memory with Stu: "Oh my God! Look! It's where I shot my film!" But he was not there, and there was no one to share this memory with. There was absolutely nobody in the world for whom this experience had any relevance whatsoever. What had once been a joyful shared experience became a haunting, isolating one.

There is a lifetime of these recollections and associations. And while some argue that at least there are the memories, and this is true to some extent, it offers little comfort to find one's self completely, utterly and absolutely unable to share and reflect on them with the person who was integral to their architecture. Moreover, there is now no one at all to share such memories with.

Part of one's self is erased when one's partner dies.

If we accept that who we are sits somewhere within the interplay of our social, psychological and biological being, then the loss of a loved one affects our identity in a profound way. As well as the emotional aspect of grief and loss, there is a 'neuro-physiological' element to it that is as real as the physical reality of the life and clinical death of the spouse.

The bereaved person's personal reality is redefined as he or she adapts to the absence of the other, adjusting to a life in which the other person no longer has a physical presence. The circuitry of the brain must be rewired as it disconnects from the presence of the other, to establish a new connection that is based upon the absence of the other.

This adjustment is life-changing: we don't just 'get on with our lives', we don't simply 'move on' as if we have just shifted house or changed jobs. In fact, we must make enormous adjustments to this physical, emotional and psycho-physiological (or neuro-physiological as mentioned before) change that has taken place in our lives. We must create a place for this change, and integrate it into a completely new sense of personal reality.

What is the nature of this change? In what ways is this new definition and experience of personal reality different from the reality of before? What is it like? How does one adapt to this new world? How do we just 'move on' and 'get over it' as others implore us to do, all the while with the imprint of a shared history etched firmly into our hearts? How do we master the balancing act of being present to life in the moment, yet staying true to who we once were, that is, the person whose reality was once enmeshed in the reality of another? Or perhaps we do change; perhaps we do become someone else. As independent and individual as our previous sense of self may have been, this identity was nevertheless in relation to the specific dynamic implicit in the broader context of the relationship, and it is this very dynamic itself that vanishes when one of the two voices within it falls silent.

This book seeks, in some small measure, to ease the excruciating alienation and loss that bereavement brings very simply by sharing personal stories. Storytelling casts light on the richness and depth of the human condition, and can help bring healing in that, through sharing our stories, we see that others have walked a similar path. It can be a tremendous solace to know that although one's journey is unique, one is not necessarily alone. In sharing our stories, we are united in a collective bond of humanity, and our stories, in turn, become a celebration of life.

The stories of loss and hope which follow celebrate the human journey, honouring the lives of the people who are no longer with us, the men and women who must carry their memories alone, and the enduring capacity of the spirit which gently and persistently helps broken hearts to mend.

1

Pilgrimage

The Soul's decent into the Night of Darkness is a harrowing experience. It is as if our very core is shattered, savagely torn apart with razor sharp shrapnel piercing through flesh and bone. We are dragged, kicking and screaming, into a living nightmare from which we cannot wake.

Our journey back towards the land of the living is a treacherous one that demands of its travellers absolute fidelity: we are spared nothing of its gruelling and relentless forward march into the harsh glare of a naked, brutal daylight.

And when we pause momentarily for life-giving oxygen, looking about to discern our whereabouts, our breath is snatched away once again as we find ourselves in completely unfamiliar surroundings. Unable to see where we are for the grit in our eyes, our bearings all but lost, we stand on unsteady ground, our feet straining for some place solid on which to rest.

Without some solid place on which to rest and without our centre we no longer recognise who we are.

As we no longer know who we are, we can longer be who we once were.

Sifting through the ashes of the life that once was, we look for evidence of who we may have been, finding fragments of ourselves in another lifetime – snapshots in time, bric-a-brac, familiar haunts and favourite songs, all tugging at heartstrings torn and bleeding from this severing of flesh.

Bandages are applied to stem an endless flow of blood. Wiping smiles across our faces to disguise our wretched truths and tortured anguish, we ghost our way through each new day on autopilot, never really showing up for muster.

Well-meaning friends trot out metered doses of welfare checks, yet go about their lives as if nothing has really changed. "Nothing has changed?" we rail. "Are you blind?"

Sheltered behind rose coloured glasses that conceal a multitude of inconvenient truths, these 'well-meaners' tiptoe gingerly around our broken bones. Too close a proximity to the wounded may prove fatal: Death, it seems, is catching!

With time's passage, the raw edge of death's harrowing presence softens. Slowly, almost imperceptibly, something miraculous begins to take place. Where heartstrings were ruptured, a fibrous sinew of scar tissue forms, thickening and strengthening over the place where the open wound once was.

Our faint and tremulous heartbeat begins to grow stronger. Though it can never fully heal, blood flow is less constricted, and precious life-giving oxygen flows freely to the thirsty, life-

hungry soul-body. If you listen very carefully, you can hear the beat that the heart skips where it once kept time with The Other.

Now we stand on our own two feet. We are tall; we have grown strong. The world we now inhabit is a changed place where rules are unfamiliar and fellow players like strangers.

We have only the tiny navigational tools found in the melancholic echo of our heart's song to guide us in this place. With these tools, we learn to move bravely into this New World, head upright, eyes looking in the direction we travel.

Within our hearts, a dizzying feat of juggling takes place: a fragile balance is held between that sacred space occupied by the Other, and the space that is responsive to the footprints of the new.

It is said that time is the great healer. We know differently. Without sacred space (that place in our hearts where our loved ones live) time is but an empty vacuum, a moment without meaning, a line between cradle and grave.

Through our pilgrimage we learn that it is in the dance between the spaces in time and place that the spark of life is rekindled, and spirit can find in us once more a house to claim as home.

2

Star-Crossed Lovers:
the meeting

Those of us fortunate to emerge into adulthood unscathed by childhood trauma will most likely find ourselves compelled towards a life bound by the influences of tradition and social expectation. We are enticed from the shelter of the family home into the adventures beckoning us in the unexplored world beyond.

Along the way, if we are lucky, we will have danced with curiosity, flirted with passion, and discovered sufficient challenge in the trials of daily life to forge character into our emergent identity.

Somewhere along our life's journey we paint ourselves into a picture that invariably has at its centre the loved one, and perhaps, the creation of our own family as its core.

It is a magical time when the stars in the heavens conspire to bring two souls into orbit with each other, allowing the intersection of two paths to create a shared destiny.

21

The Photograph

There is a photograph.
In it, there is a young man with long shiny brown hair,
and a young woman, slightly older than he,
She too has long hair, the shade of mousey brown
that blonde turns into as it matures from childhood
to young adult.
She plays to the camera, striking a pose.
An aspiring actress, she seizes the opportunity to play
to this impersonal audience.
He looks into the lens of the camera giggling
self-consciously at their play.
Peels of laughter ring out from behind the curtain
of the booth in which they sit.
Their portrait is captured and a moment in time
distilled, the quintessence of eternal youth.
Through her eyes she sees a world of hope
and promise,
life and love as yet untarnished by the passage of time.
Alive. Living.
Life is joyous, uncomplicated, exciting,
a continual triumph of exuberance over the constriction
of a more pedestrian circumstance.
His hands hold her,
brown and strong, long fingers wrapped around her,
arms gentle yet firm,
his eyes, dark brown and mysterious,
gentle, warm and loving.

There seems to be a wisdom beyond the
possessor's years;
an old soul come to visit,
perhaps only for a short time,
will he inhabit this young handsome body.
Through his eyes, he sees an adventurous path
awaiting them.
He is certain he will make her his Bride.

Conversations

BEV BROCK

Bev and Peter Brock were no strangers to the public eye. Rising to prominence with his talent for motor sports in the 1970s, a charismatic Peter Brock was proudly embraced by Australians as their home grown motor racing legend, King of the Mountain. Peter's public success as a motor racing great was complemented by the family life created at home by Bev and him.

Although separated at the time of his passing, their deep affection and love for one another was a bond that distance had in no way diminished. Here, Bev recalls the occasion when she and Peter met.

Peter and I met back in the early seventies. I was married to another guy at that time who dabbled in motor racing. His best mate was Peter's mechanic. Peter was married to Michelle, who was the then Miss Australia. Meanwhile, I was a very simple girl from a country town in Western Australia who had never lived the high life, or ever known anything about it. In those days Peter was sort of 'there', he had won his first Bathurst, and he was on his way, but at the time he was going through a very messy marriage breakdown.

Peter didn't have much money, certainly not from motor racing, and so when they came and raced in Sydney they would come and stay with us, and they'd have free meals, free board, and we'd be pit crew for them as well. I was always referred to as Mother Earth back then and regarded as a good listener, and we struck up a sound friendship. He felt completely safe about talking about the mess that was his life at that time.

And so for the first couple of years that I knew him, we were friends and I was counselling him through a very rough patch in his life, while at the same time trying to make my own marriage work. We became firm friends, and I guess there was mutual respect built up over that time. What I saw was not what other people saw. For a public person, he was very private. He kept his private stuff to himself, and I was one of the few people he opened up to. What I saw was this man with incredible talent who could achieve anything, yet who, in fact, was so vulnerable and so wounded that he wasn't moving on with his life.

I finally got to the point when I couldn't make my marriage work any more, and I essentially gave up trying. It was only when I said that the marriage was over that Peter acknowledged how he felt about me.

I have to say that even through my pregnancy Peter was

infinitely closer to that baby than my then husband had been. We were very good friends before we got together, and so we had a very stable start to our relationship. He became the instant father to a six-month-old boy. That's not easy for a lot of young men but he was exceptional, he was just incredible, and our relationship went from strength to strength.

A lot of people tried to warn me off the relationship because he was seen to be a womaniser who was a motor racing driver and not very responsible, whereas I was exactly the other way, the one who was stable and so my family thought I'd gone crazy. They were living in Western Australia, and they never knew of the dramas I'd been having in my life and all they saw was this very stable girl who had flipped out and run off with a racing car driver. But the reality was very different, and we went on to have twenty-eight years of the most amazing relationship. We were the best of friends, and we talked about absolutely everything. It would be fair to say that people saw the public side of Peter as one thing, a public person with a high profile, a racing driver of enormous success, whereas I saw something completely different.

He couldn't do everything on his own, and I guess I gave him a sense of stability and security that enabled him to go and do all the things he did. He left me to take care of all the so-called 'little things' like dealing with bank managers and accountants and solicitors and running the home and raising the kids. These were the 'little things' while he went off and did the big things, like race cars, because as he said he could not possibly have had his career and had to take care of all the other things as well.

So we were the yin and yang, we both brought skills and talent to the relationship and we were committed to making it work. We had both been married before, and weren't interested in a formal marriage again because we both knew that didn't necessarily make a partnership work. A lot of people didn't understand our relationship because he was very attractive to women and they made no bones about the fact that they were after him. I was not a jealous or possessive person which is probably why the relationship lasted so long, but I had absolute faith in the way he loved the kids and me. He would always say to me, "Bev, I couldn't live without you."

KERRI NEWLAND

Kerri lives in the outer suburbs of Melbourne keeping busy with her three children. As a young woman, Kerri worked part-time at a local fish and chip shop frequented by her future husband, career fire fighter and carpenter, Jeff Newland.

I went to a party one Saturday night with my boyfriend at the time who was probably not an ideal partner, but good fun and we met up with his friends and friends of friends. Jeff was at this party. I had met him several times before at various different places and had got along quite well with him. We were having a friendly chat on this one occasion at this party and he said to me, "I'm going to marry you one day!" Feeling a little embarrassed, I just sort of let it roll over me and continued partying. He had made another hint to me at a park a few weeks earlier that I thought I must have misunderstood. Being seventeen at the time, I had very little confidence in myself.

I used to work part time in the local fish and chip shop, and I remember him bringing in his brother and his brother's girlfriend one day, and he later told me that he had brought them into the shop to show them the girl he was going to marry someday. He used to joke that I used to give him extra potato cakes, so how could he pass that up. I joked that he must have got the wrong order!

My boyfriend and I eventually split up, much to my mum and dad's delight, and Jeff was waiting there on the sidelines. We talked on the telephone a few times and then went on our first date down to Mt. Martha for the day. We had a great day at the beach, just getting to know each other.

Our first night out together was at Rembrandt's with a friend of his and his fiancé. When we decided that we would get married, Jeff formally proposed at the Regent Hotel in the city, where we had lunch. It was very romantic. We combined my twenty-first birthday celebration with our engagement, having a small party at my parents' home with about sixty guests.

Jeff and I were married on the 25th of November 1989, at St. John's Anglican Church in Diamond Creek, opposite a block of land that we had already bought. Jeff was a carpenter by trade, and we were looking forward to building our dream home.

Our wedding day came around soon enough and we were graced with a beautiful warm, sunny day. On entering the church I was full of excitement, which surprised me, because I was usually very emotional at weddings. I could see, to my surprise, a very nervous groom waiting for me at the altar.

Our day was enjoyed by everyone but most especially the bride and groom! That night, we stayed at the Regent Hotel, where Jeff had proposed. The next morning we flew to Sydney and then the following morning on to Fiji. It was the first holiday we had together and it was wonderful. We enjoyed our honeymoon to the full, socialising with other newlyweds, scuba diving, snorkelling, and generally just totally relaxing. We returned just before Christmas and moved into a rented unit in Greensborough. It was very basic, but it was cheap. This also motivated us to save money so we could get on with building our own home.

Jeff was also a career fire fighter for the Metropolitan Fire Brigade and was stationed at Eastern Hill in the city. He loved his job, hanging out with all the boys on his shift. Unless it was the weekend, he worked carpentry on his days off. Our days were spent visiting family and friends, checking out local markets, and having friends over for drinks and dinner.

I couldn't believe that I married a fire fighter who worked shift work! I hated staying on my own overnight, and never had stayed alone, so I used to stay at my mum and dad's for the two nights and later on in the marriage, one night at my mum's and one night at his mum's. We moved into our dream home about two years after we married. We were thrilled. We had no front door, as the living areas were all upstairs, so we had to walk around to the back door to enter. Eventually we used a ladder up to the front of the house. We had an extension cord to a power pole for power, an open fireplace for heating, and there was no carpet or tiles, but we felt like a king and queen.

My brother-in-law organised carpet tiles for our living areas made up of samples and off- cuts, and each one was different, but it didn't matter to us; to us it was luxury! We knew our home would soon be completed so we barely even noticed these problems.

In 1993, we went overseas to Egypt, the UK and Europe for six weeks with my sister and brother-in-law. It was a quick decision but a fantastic experience. We had an absolute ball. Jeff really loved the historical background of England, Scotland and Wales. We even visited the house where his dad had lived as a child.

In 1995, our first child, Sarah Louise Newland was born four weeks early and was delivered by emergency caesarean. She barely weighed five pounds. Unfortunately they dented her skull in delivery and the next morning she was sent over to the Royal Children's Hospital to have her skull repaired. I was in the Frances Perry House, and Jeff was looking after all the arrangements for Sarah. It was a very emotional time. She was born on a Thursday and wasn't back with me until the following Tuesday. Jeff organised for me to visit Sarah at the Children's on the Saturday and Sunday so I could bond with her. Luckily, as she was our first baby and everything was new to us, we did not realise what a trauma we were facing. Somehow we coped well and everything worked out all right. Jeff was very much the doting father.

Liam Thomas Newland was born in 1999. His was a very easy arrival with a planned caesarean. Jeff relished looking after Sarah on his own, bringing her into the city to see me every day. He even took Sarah to the zoo by tram before visiting me, returning with a stuffed lion and tiger for Liam.

Our children were growing up too quickly and after some debating as to whether to have another baby or not, we were blessed with another pregnancy in 2003, with the arrival date just after Jeff's fortieth birthday.

Jeff had also started a new project with a friend from the fire brigade; they were to build two new homes to sell. They had bought the land and were busy organising all the plans and finer details. He was very excited about all this as he felt as though he was really working for himself and enjoying the rewards of being his own boss. Now he had the best of both worlds.

LINDA BURNEY

A keen advocate for Indigenous Peoples' issues in the New South Wales Department of Aboriginal Affairs, Linda's ascent through the ranks of Australian public life conceals a parallel journey that presents perhaps far greater challenges than those of a successful career in Australian politics.

A shared passion and commitment to their work was a defining strength of her relationship with Rick Farley, former Executive Director of the National Farmers' Union.

Rick and I were both professionals and both had very independent successful lives before we became partners, and we met each other later in life. I was forty-five, which would make him about forty-nine. We both spent a lot of time in aeroplanes, particularly Rick, and one of the great things about our relationship is that there wasn't any angst or jealousy or any, "Don't tell me you are going away again!" or the stuff that often bedevils relationships where there is extensive separation or travel by one or both partners. And that was what was just fantastic about our relationship: there was absolute trust and understanding that that in fact was what our political lives were about.

We had a second sense of each other in terms of politics and understanding of what the political realm required of people, of what it took of people, and what was great about it was we just knew. We didn't have to go through all those things that many relationships go through when in the media, or dealing with politicians, or politics, or difficult situations.

Rick was a very singular person and it took me a long time to get to understand that. He was not a big talker, and it took a while to get used to the fact that there were not long periods of pillow talk, or that you had to be deep and meaningful all the time otherwise somehow your relationship was not working. We didn't have that angst there. It didn't mean we didn't have great discussions and long talks, it just meant that neither of us felt the need to divulge everything about our thoughts and our past lives. We didn't do any of that kind of stuff, it was all a given.

ROSE BENNETT

Rose has two children and works as a librarian in the outer suburbs of Melbourne. For the younger Rose, the world was a place of adventure and romance, and the man who would take centre stage in her life was someone she had admired from a distance before becoming romantically involved with him.

The Andrew I met was wonderful. He was beautiful. He was calm and strong and had such an inner beauty about him. He was intelligent, and one of the things I loved about him was his wit. He had an amazing sense of humour.

How we met was funny; we kept on crossing paths. He was studying at university at the time, and he would be getting on a tram, and I would be getting off and we would bump into each other over and over again. He'd just smile at me with his beautiful eyes. Over time we became friends, good friends, and then finally we became romantically involved. Eventually we were married, and had two beautiful children.

For Andrew and me, life wasn't planned out. We were happy to take things one day at a time. It made him happy that way. In fact he was at his happiest then, as was I. When starting a relationship, you're never really sure where you're going to wind up, you just trust that life will unfold as it is meant to. And then when you marry, you think it's going to be for life. When we met, I remember, I felt as if our path was not going to be an easy one. But I was okay with that; I would just take it one day at a time. We had each other, we had our children: things were good. And that was all that mattered.

JUNE BUCK

June suspects her passion for the theatre is something she inherited from her husband, David. Their journey began in Essex, a county in East England, at a time when people met one another face to face, and where teenagers could walk home from being out on a date, safe on the streets at night.

When I was a girl we used to have carnivals that would travel around the countryside, and each and every year the carnival would come to our local park. And there'd be swings and merry-go-rounds and all these wonderful things. It was a bit like Luna Park, but on a smaller scale.

One particular Saturday, my girlfriend and I were supposed to be going to a party but it was cancelled at the last minute, and we were all dolled up in our beautiful outfits: our hair was done, our high heel shoes were on, you know, all nice new clothes. And we thought, "Oh, what are we going to do now? It's Saturday night, we're all dressed up, and there's nowhere to go!"

We knew that the fair was on so we caught the bus and went into Barking, in Essex, which was my hometown, and went to the carnival. My girlfriend met a boy she was sort of going out with, but I didn't get along with his friend. It was mutual, and I wasn't about to go out with them for the sake of my friend, and so I thought it was better that I went home.

In those days it was safe for teenagers to be walking around in the streets. You could walk home on your own. But she wouldn't have any of it. She didn't want me going home on my own. In the meantime there was a crowd of boys that we sort of knew, and she said to me, "Oh, I know him! I'll get him to walk you home!" And she goes up to a particular boy and asks him to walk me home, and he agreed to. When we arrived home, he asked if he could see me the next day. I said yes.

So the next day he came around, and I introduced him to my parents, and later when we said goodnight, he said, "I'm going to marry you!" (I was sixteen at the time, by the way. He would have been nineteen, possibly twenty.) I thought, "I don't think so! I've too much to do!"

But we did. We did eventually get married. It was two years before we got engaged, and then it was two years later that we got married.

In England, you're twenty-one when you get the 'key of the door' as they called it, and that's when you can get married without your parents' permission. Girls did, of course, but it was the way things were supposed to happen back then. If you wanted to get married, you waited until you were twenty-one.

And so, I got married at twenty-one. I was twenty-one in June, and we got married in October, and then two years later we came out to Australia. David's parents were here and his two sisters were here. He was the last one in his family who had wanted to come over here.

We didn't know at the time if we would stay here permanently. We came out on the ten pound scheme, and it was stipulated that you had to stay here for two years. If you stayed two years you could go back on the ten-pound scheme, but if you decided to go back before the two years were up you had to pay for your fare back. We stayed of course.

We were very lucky because David's parents and his sisters wrote to us and they didn't paint the pavement with gold; they told us exactly how things were here, what it was like, what to expect, so we were very lucky. We had somewhere to come to when we came out. David's parents lived in Eltham; they had just built their home, and so we went and lived with them.

David found a block of land in a neighbouring suburb, for us to build our house on. We stayed with his mum and dad for nearly two years, because in those days you had to buy your land before you could build on it. Things are different now, obviously, but back then you had to finish paying for it. So we stayed with David's mum, and I went to work, he went to work, and we eventually paid off the land, and then we built our house.

You don't have brick veneers in England, there it's all double brick, and so to build a house like this was quite an experience. We had a bricklayer, a plumber, and an electrician, but all the rest, all the woodwork, David built. He made the frames at work, and then they brought them up here and put them up. We lived in a caravan in the carport for a little while. We had Paul at the time, he was just a little baby, and Jodie came along later.

David was my buddy; he was my husband; he was my best friend. He was also my backstop, especially when it came to the theatre – we belonged to the local Theatre Company – because I wasn't as confident as he was. He was very confident, and he was just fantastic on stage. He had a charisma about him, and he captured the audience's attention. He would grab them and pull them in to him. He was a wonderful performer. I was very nervous on stage, but he would always say to me, "You'll be good, you'll be fine!" I'd say, "Now, what about if I do this?" and he'd say, "Yeah, that'd be good, that'd work." And I'd ask, "Should I change it?" And he would reassure me, "No just leave it; just get up there. You'll be fine."

Right before a show, I would be pacing the dressing room, up and down, up and down, but not David. He would just walk around, so blasé, so matter of fact. And then it would be time for him to go onstage and he would get out there and just shine! He would just shine! I had done a couple of sketches with him, which was great, but I never thought I had enough talent to act or to be next to him because he was so talented. He was just a natural. He'd been on the stage since he was a kid. He was a very good tap dancer. He was also in two quartets, and he would go around to nursing homes and retirement villages during the day with the daytime quartet and he would sing for the residents.

David was my confidence. He was my backstop.

ELWYN GONSALVEZ

Elwyn keeps busy looking after his three kids, working for the railways, playing competitive tennis and also volunteering as a fire fighter. His romance with Cathy began at the local roller skating rink after the girl Elwyn had hoped to skate with had other plans.

Cathy and I first met at high school. She was a good friend and a classmate of my younger sister. I was invited to a roller skating party by a girl I intended to ask out, however to my surprise she had a new boyfriend. Naturally I was disappointed and was sitting down when Cathy spotted me. She came up to me, extended her hand and asked if I would like to skate with her, which I did for most of the night. The next day she called to say thank you and that she had a really good time. I was then invited to go ice-skating with some of her friends the following week, which was when we had our first kiss. Cathy was sixteen years old at the time, and told me that when she first met me she thought I was really good looking. She reckons that she had had a crush on me since she was twelve, and couldn't believe that we were finally going out!

Two weeks later she asked me to marry her! We got engaged when she was seventeen, and then married at nineteen. I was twenty-three at the time.

We were a very loyal and affectionate couple. Even after several years of marriage, we would often still hold hands when walking together. It was common for us to fall asleep in each other's arms. Cathy would put her head on my chest because she said she liked hearing my heartbeat, and I would be able to smell the scent of her hair. It always smelled so sweet.

PAUL SAID

Paul Said is a shift worker who lives in regional Victoria. On the recommendation of the local priest, he placed a notice in the personal section of a local Catholic paper, and was set on a path towards a life with his future wife, Delina.

I was twenty-seven years old at the time and living in Newborough in the Latrobe Valley with my parents. I had had girlfriends on and off for quite some years, but they were just that, 'friends'. I was concerned that I may never meet someone who could be more than just a friend.

Father Cusack was our local parish priest and very much like a second father to me because I could talk to him openly about any subject. One day at church I said to him, "Father, I am having trouble finding the girl of my dreams." He replied to me half jokingly, "Put a notice in *The Messenger*!" *The Messenger* was a Catholic magazine that came out once a month. The back few pages were reserved for Pen Friends and people wishing to meet their soul mate. So I put my notice in *The Messenger*, going under the pen name of Ron and it was printed in the following month's edition.

In due course I received three replies, two from a couple of ladies whose names I have forgotten, and then one from a lady by the name of Delina who lived in Sydney. Delina wrote me a beautiful letter and also sent me her photo. I replied to all three ladies but the other two did not reply. Delina, however, did reply. Her writing was meticulous, neat and perfect and had a way of drawing me in to the letter.

We corresponded for about two months, writing to each other at least once a week. I finally worked up enough courage and asked her if I could come to Sydney to meet her, to which she agreed. We arranged a time and a date.

I drove all the way to Sydney the night before the day we had arranged to meet each other. I booked into the Greystanes Inn, which was not too far from our arranged meeting place. I had a shower and nervously waited for the time to arrive to meet her.

The meeting time drew nearer and even more nervously, I drove to her mother's place where we arranged to meet. I arrived too early but I could not wait so I knocked on the front door. It was Delina who opened the door. I couldn't believe this vision before me! She took my breath away! She invited me in and my immediate thoughts were that I didn't have a chance with this beautiful young lady. Delina introduced me to her mother. This made me even more nervous, however Delina did most of the talking at first and somehow I felt relaxed and comfortable in her presence.

The way in which we Delina and I met was truly an act of God, as Delina was not Catholic and at the time when my notice was printed in *The Messenger*, and she was a two and a half hour drive away from her house, staying at her girlfriend's place in Lither. Her friend Mary just happened to be Catholic and just happened to have that copy of *The Messenger* and was reading it at the time. Mary was going through the notices in the back pages and came across my notice. It was Mary who talked Delina into answering my notice.

I knew straight away that Delina was the one for me.

We wrote to and visited each other for about three months. Delina was down visiting me in Melbourne once and we had arranged to go to the beach for the day. On the drive back home I stopped the car in the middle of nowhere. I very nervously said, "I have something to ask you." I was shaking and felt extremely nervous. I said, "Delina, will you marry me?" After a few brief seconds of silence Delina replied, "I'll have to think about it." I was crushed. Nothing else was mentioned about my question all day. Later, I drove Delina to the airport for her return flight to Sydney. Still nothing was mentioned. I was feeling pretty low.

The next day, I received a telegram from Delina simply saying, "Yes to your question." I was over the moon and could not wait to tell my friends and family.

After a short engagement we were married at the Holy Trinity Catholic Church in Granville in Sydney. It was truly a fairytale romance and a marriage made in heaven. Delina gave me thirty-one years and one glorious day of fantastic married life.

For medical reasons, we were not able to have children. This was very hard for both of us to accept, as we both had wanted a family of our own. But Delina and I never looked back. If we couldn't have a family of our own, at least we had each other. We were truly devoted to one another, always surprising each other with little gifts; wherever we went we always held hands; we loved and respected each other and seemed always to sense what the other was thinking. I loved just being near Delina. She was my whole life.

Delina worked full time for a few years. I was on shift

work at the time and often we would sometimes miss each other, as I would be starting my shift when Delina was finishing her day's work. We would always leave each other little notes with happenings of the day's events. I would always have the housework and the cooking done for her so she could rest when she got home from work.

Delina was truly the best part of my life. I often think back to the humble beginning of how we met and what a truly beautiful relationship became of that insignificant notice in *The Messenger*.

ERIKA SCHWARTZ

It was while working abroad that Erika first met Damian, her future husband. Living in a Central New South Wales farming community, Erika masters the act of balancing family and work commitments while studying for her PhD in Middle Eastern Politics.

We first met at a Hamas rally in Palestine. The Israelis had deported Hamas members and dumped them in the hills across the border in Lebanon. We were both watching a rally protesting the deportations at the university where I worked, and Damian, having recently arrived, asked me what was going on. He had long wavy hair, and he was just himself in all the strangeness around us. It is painful to think about all the years that we could have been together had we managed to seize the opportunity back then. If only I had known him then as I knew him later, when we were together in his environment.

When we finally were together for good, we didn't waste time. Our two boys were born; we moved to the country; we concentrated on family; we spent as much time together as we could. We didn't do much separately; we wanted to be together. I phoned him at work few times each day, and when I saw the ute pull up in front of the house, I couldn't wait for him to step through the door. My older boy remembers him building Duplo aeroplanes with him, lying on the floor. He was physical and hands-on with the boys, and a natural at parenting. I never, ever, even for a second, doubted my choice of him. And I felt okay about parenting because I knew he was there, and all would be good.

Five years, that's all we had together here in this country. We didn't take being together for granted, and strangely, I always felt I hadn't had enough time with him, even when he was still alive and we had no idea that time was running out. He was good with people, had a gentleness towards and real interest in them. He accepted them as they were and didn't try to change them. I often felt that I needed to learn his skill with people. He never pushed me into changing my mind, but accepted me, and in time, without pressure, but with a better understanding that comes with time and familiarity, I often came around to his preferred choice – like his preference for living here in the countryside, near his family. He never pushed, he just waited.

When I drive out to the farm where Damian grew up, I can see him in the land. I love that land – dry, rough, beautiful, and entirely without pretence. When I first met Damian I didn't know any of this. It took years to finally make the decision to be together in the same country. I know now that to understand him meant to see where he came from: "East of Cocoparra, where my people live." Seeing this land is to understand him; his quiet nature, his love of family, his physical strength, his restfulness, his stubbornness, and his resilience, and also his acceptance of people, of me, and of fate.

ANN RATTLEY

Ann Rattley is a clinical psychologist based in Melbourne whose work in the field sometimes reveals a darker side of the human condition. It was while working in corporate training that she first met Patrick, a Vietnam War veteran.

I was at a two-day training seminar for work, and this guy came in late and I thought, "Hmm! You look interesting." He was an absolute presence. He was amazing. And I remember what he was wearing too: he had on his red fireman braces, grey trousers and a blue shirt. And apparently he noticed me straight away too, because he said to me later, "I saw you and thought to myself, 'Here's the woman I've been looking for, for thirty years'." So we were kind of aware of each other straight away. And it was one of those training courses where they put things on your name tag – like different coloured stickers – and at the break when you go and sit with all the people with pink stickers or whatever and he'd changed the stickers so that we ended up sitting together. It was quite funny.

At the end of the next day, we caught a cab back in to town. I generalised the offer to some of the others, but typical Patrick, he pulled a face because it was all or nothing for him. I just assumed that if he wanted to talk to me he'd wait until the end of the cab ride when the others had gone. I was a little bit nervous of jumping in a cab with him, but in the end we wound up taking that cab ride back into town.

That was in October, and then I did some management training and he offered to come up with the proposals for each job I was working on and so we kept in contact through work for about six months and it took about six months until we got together. We had each been living with different people at that time, and we had both broken up with those people coincidentally, and so we met for coffee. He was so full on. I wasn't used to someone being that full on and really interested.

We started going out in May, and six weeks later in July he asked me to marry him. And I think my first words were "Shit," and my second words were, "Jesus Christ," and I didn't answer him for another six weeks. He asked in July and I answered in early September by phone from London. And we'd only started going out in late May.

We were both pretty intense, which wasn't always a good mix. We both had a fairly reasonable sense of the ridiculous, he even more so than I. We were both opposites in some ways and similar in others. He was very 'big picture' and grandiose about things and had lots of ideas and I was always focussed on the details. There's no point running into a forest if you can't see the trees because you'll just crash into them. I'm seeing the trees that you've got to run around, whereas he was like, "Oh no, it'll be alright!"

He was very playful. He'd do things like he did on one occasion when we were walking down the street in the city, back where Allan's Music used to be, and I remember there was a Frank Sinatra song booming out of the shop, I think it was, *New York, New York*, and he grabbed me and started dancing down the street with me. And I couldn't dance. And I was feeling pretty silly, but he was swept up with great passion and excitement and fun.

He was very loyal, something of a homebody in lots of ways. We liked pottering around a lot. I think that for him it was very different to have someone who wanted to potter around with him, because he didn't have that experience with his first wife at all. And I would do things like drag him out on picnics, and he hadn't been on picnics before. And I taught him to sleep in, and read the paper in bed and have breakfast in bed, or not breakfast so much as coffee in bed with the paper. There was a lot of togetherness. We might go to a party or something and we'd end up being in a corner and just chatting like we'd just met and we were really interested in what each other had to say. This whole party would be going on around us we'd be just chatting to one another. We used to really enjoy that. It was as if we weren't really at the party even though we were there.

We were both a bit melancholic, I think. It was just hard. We had such a dreadful time financially with work. It was the toughest of marriages from that point of view. And I didn't know that he had PTSD (post traumatic stress disorder) until a couple of years into the relationship. It was to do with the War. With Vietnam. He was like a lot of veterans in that they come back from the war and they need to do something similar or with immediacy and with adrenalin, problem solving and all that sort of stuff. They can't just go and sit at a desk job and be normal and drive cabs or something, so a lot of them end up in the police force or as *fireys* or *ambos*. So he was a *firey* after a while, but not at the time we met.

I didn't know about the stress disorder for some time, so that added a dimension to our relationship. He used to have nightmares, and there were a number of instructions about when he was sleeping, like not to touch his face, and if I had to wake him up at any time I was only to shake his foot gently. He used to sleep with his hand underneath the pillow, which was where he had kept his gun.

Eventually we got to the point where I could elbow him when he was snoring, and tell him to breathe because he had sleep apnoea. Or there'd be occasions such as when I'd want to go to the movies, but he wouldn't want to, and it was only later that I found out that there were times that he couldn't go into a cinema or places like that because he couldn't be in a dark, enclosed space, where he was out of control, with people behind him. In such places he was not able to control his environment. But I didn't know any of this. I knew nothing about the PTSD at the time. There I was just thinking he was being lazy not wanting to go to the pictures with me. So it wasn't easy; our marriage definitely wasn't easy from that point of view.

In conversation with another veteran one time, we concluded that there are two types of combat vets – ones who had been involved in the kind of operations that Patrick and he had been, and then the rest. While others had their own troubles, those who had been involved in these types of operations and had experienced certain things that, if they had survived, created an edge, and in Patrick's case, it had created an extra depth, a kind of guardedness and silence about him.

PAUL BELFRAGE

Paul works in the disability services and shares his home in outer metropolitan Melbourne with his four children. A keen musician, Paul plays the saxophone in a jazz band and it was during a stay in the country, prior to commencing formal music studies, that his path crossed with Leanne's.

Leanne and I met in Sale in East Gippsland in October 1985. She was starting a job at a training centre for Christian youth workers. I was living at the centre for a short while before returning to Melbourne to start musical studies. I really wasn't looking for a partner, or to fall in love. In fact, I was not sure how things would go between us once I returned to Melbourne. I had been pretty burned out a few years earlier and was in Gippsland for time out, as well as to help with building my retired parents' new house in one of the neighbouring towns.

I remember, early one evening the secretary requested assistance for a young lady with her luggage that needed to be taken to one of the upstairs rooms of the house. I went outside and picked up a brown wooden trunk (which our youngest, now twelve years old, has in her room) and took it up for our new administration assistant. There may have been a little flirting going on, but I didn't really think anything of it. Little did I know at the time that Leanne had taken quite a shine to me.

I will never forget the night we made that everlasting connection. On a summer's night shortly after Leanne's arrival, I went to the old gym and started to play my saxophone. I was so engrossed in the sound it made in that space that I hadn't noticed Leanne standing there watching me. She later told me she felt the music had called to her, that she felt drawn to it. We talked for hours, sharing much of ourselves that night. It was captivating and seductive: we were both young, we were in this beautiful rural setting with three hundred acres of lush green dairy property, staggering sunsets, and romantic scenery.

I loved Leanne so very much. I fell so hard and so totally for her. She knew who I was. Her intuition and her heart were her most amazing gifts to us, her family, as well as to her community. She would always have a moment and an ear to spare. She wanted to meet and learn from anyone who came into her life. Creating a sense of community was so important to her.

We shared a love of art, language, music, philosophy, teaching, dance, the outdoors and theatre. I was into jazz and Leanne enjoyed listening and learning about it from me. We both had a wacky side and would ham it up for each other as often as possible. At my fortieth birthday, we dressed up as Beauty and the Beast, and I played a set of jazz tunes with a few jazz *musos* I knew, and I wore a crazy monster mask. We did a few workshops in clowning and had a ball, and even floated the idea of doing a kids' party business together.

As first time parents of a very colicky baby, we became creative in trying to relieve his wailing and stress by taking the three of us out for a drive. The benefits were that Danny sat up, had a distraction, and burped himself, while we got to talk, to spend time with each other and catch up. It was like a mini date. As Dan fell asleep, we parked the car at the Fitzroy Gardens and sat on the grass four metres away with a coffee, one eye (or ear) on the baby, the other on each other. We always wanted to be close, physically and emotionally.

There is a particular photograph that I took of Leanne on one of our many 'at home dates' that I love to revisit. We planned our lovely date as friends offered to babysit our two eldest, which would leave us with our third child, twelve-month-old Jay. We shopped, moved the dining table into the lounge room from the kitchen and set it with flowers from the garden, our very best cutlery and a couple of wine glasses. We cooked dinner for little Jay and then made our own special meal, hurried up to our room to dress for each other, and then raced back to put finishing touches to the menu.

My photograph of Leanne that night captured a softness and a beauty about her which I will always treasure. She wore a lovely deep blue evening dress, her long hair flowing down in sandstone-coloured spiral lengths, her face showing her tiredness from taking care of our children, yet wanting to nurture our love and romance as well. We danced, told stories, and laughed. We looked after baby Jay and then put him to bed. And made love. A simple night filled with the joy of simply having her in my life, and it lives on in my memory as one of the sweetest.

3

Dark Night of the Soul: when hope is shattered and the nightmare begins

The Beauty of the world has two edges, one of laughter, one of anguish, cutting the world asunder.

A Room of One's Own, Virginia Woolf

And so our journeys transpire. Families extend, new generations emerge, and life stories, built up incrementally over many years, move inexorably towards their conclusion.

However sometimes life does not unfold the way we think it will. Illness, divorce, the loss of a job, a workplace accident, drought, fire, flood - myriad unexpected events can become disruptive undercurrents in our lives wreaking havoc and throwing us off our path.

The death of our partner or spouse is like a tidal wave of destruction that severs our world in two and casts us adrift in a sea of anguish.

Journal Entry

25th August 2002

Today I have to go and view the body of my husband.

The call came in last Saturday morning. Tahn knocked on the door and said there was a bad phone call. It was Moana.

I thought she was calling about Bupcia.

It was worse.

It was Stuart.

He was dead.

Alcohol and pills.

And now it is all too late.

I have cried and wept all week.

I have been completely devastated.

I have so much to write as there is so much going on in my mind but it all races by.

They flew his body to Brisbane for an autopsy.

He made his final journey back across the continent from Brisbane to Melbourne for the last time on Friday.

He lies at a funeral parlour in Somerville.

I have been shattered many, many times in my life.

But this is truly the most shattering and devastating loss.

This last week has been hell.

This next week will be worse.

Stu.

Stu, I love you, my Stu.

Conversations

BEV

In September 2006, Australia was devastated when in the space of one week it lost two of its most celebrated icons; the infamous Crocodile Hunter and Wildlife Warrior, Steve Irwin, and the much adored Peter Brock.

News of Peter's death in a motoring accident travelled quickly across Australia. The tragic news came to Bev in a telephone call.

It was awful. It was in the afternoon and I was sitting down doing some work in the lounge room, and the phone rang, and when I answered, the caller hung up. There was nobody there and I thought it was a bit strange. About ten minutes went by and it rang, and again, the same thing. When it happened yet again I was a little bit short when I answered, and it was a motoring journalist who said to me, "Bevo, do you know there's been an accident?" I told him, "No." He said, "Peter's been in an accident and it's not good."

One of the last conversations I'd had with Peter was about the fact that he had absolutely retired. He believed it was time to give up, because he knew his timing wasn't there. He'd said to me, "Bevo, this time it is real, I am retiring. I know this time." He hadn't actually told me he was even in this day's event! So when the guy said, "Sorry to be the one to tell you, but Peter hasn't made it." I just collapsed. And then I heard the helicopters overhead and it took that short a period of time for the media to be there!

But in the meantime I had to call the kids. My nephew was living with us at the time, and I was an absolute blubbering mess. Alexandra had gone to the movies, and all I knew was that she'd gone to the Gold Class, but not which one. I couldn't stand the thought of her being told by somebody other than me. Obviously her phone was off, being at the pictures, so I had to get a girlfriend to go and track down where she was. I knew what movie she wanted to see and I knew that there were only a couple of Gold Class Cinemas, so my friend went to get her, to track down which theatre she was in and get her out of there. I had to call our middle son at work and tell him there at work, and that was just awful. He hadn't heard. And then our eldest son had heard about it on the radio. It's as though the whole world knew before we did. And nobody officially told us; ever.

And so it was a 'media' thing, and within the time that it took for the initial phone call, I had every TV station, the helicopters and everybody just descend. It was madness! When other people grieve they get to compose themselves. But, in this case, we had the whole world there, looking on, and at that stage I hadn't even been able to hug my kids. They were all in different places. Fortunately, my sister had heard. She had been at work, and so she simply left work and turned up. The neighbours had heard and they came over too. Peter's uncle, who was eighty, lived next door to us and he was like the Rock of Gibraltar. Obviously he was greatly affected by it too. The kids came, and Uncle Sandy was there and from then on, the catastrophe and its fallout just had a life of its own. I guess what helped get us through it all was the fact that our family was close and strong.

I think for me the pain was enormous, but the public scrutiny was perhaps worse. Because we had always lived in the public eye, Peter and I had had a philosophy that the media could have total access to us. He didn't like them presenting anything that wasn't true, and if they had ever had any questions, they could just call us. So he had always given out all of our phone numbers, the home numbers and our mobile numbers. This meant all the media all around Australia had access to us. And I felt that this was a time to honour his philosophy, to have that openness. It wasn't a time to go into hiding, although I would have loved to have done that.

The fact that we were separated didn't mean a thing to the media. They hadn't had anything to do with his then partner. She was being very much protected over in the West, and I didn't have that buffer. Not that I needed it to be honest, because I had been used to having to deal with the media. And they were absolutely fantastic; I have a real respect for them. They had a job to do and they were all apologetic for it.

The funeral arrangements were larger than Ben Hur. The offer to have a state funeral came in. Peter was a man for a grand affair and he'd always lived a grand life. It was what he would have wanted, and it was the only way we would have ever been able to give his fans the chance to say goodbye to him properly. We couldn't have done it any other way.

So there was a state funeral, and then we went back for a private family interment. And then a week later, well, there were a lot of big things: there was a big 'wake', if you like, up at Bathurst at the circuit there; and there was another one at Sandown (motor circuit). And so we had an ongoing series of events. Everybody felt the need to express their respect and devotion to the man, and to say their goodbyes.

Unlike a lot of people, you can't just have a funeral and it's over with. Peter's went on and on. For me it was like treading a diplomatic tightrope because whilst I wasn't his partner at the time, the public had always thought of Peter and me as a unit, and so that's where most of the attention was directed.

Then there was the media frenzy, and every day there was something more. And afterwards, just when I was thinking that everything might die down and we could get on with trying to restructure our lives, instead we had to face other hurdles. As happens with high profile people, there is always someone who wants to cut them down. There were a series of events involving public criticism, and again, as it had in the past, the media turned to me to respond to the criticisms. I had always responded in the past, and I wasn't about to stop now and let his reputation be diminished. So I was thrown into all of that. It was a tremendously challenging period.

KERRI

A new baby was due around the same time as Jeff's fortieth birthday. However, a time of celebration turned to tragedy when Jeff's work mate unexpectedly turned up on the front doorstep of Jeff and Kerri's house.

On June 23rd 2004, Jeff had a meeting with our accountant at 8.30am so I took Sarah off to school and picked up Liam's little friend for a play before taking them both to kindergarten after lunch. Jeff came back home after the meeting to sort out more paperwork, and his partner called in to discuss their timeline for the next month's building. Jeff was talking so fast! He was on a mission, and his partner had to remind him that I was booked in to have our baby on the July13th, the day before his fortieth birthday. He didn't want a party, just a quiet dinner with family, and I was thinking of organising a bit of a surprise party, but it would have to be a last minute thing.

Jeff left home at around 11am to start work on one of the new carpentry jobs in Greensborough. Liam and his friend Nicholas were busy playing and I was thinking about getting them ready for kinder in an hour or two. Our golden retriever started howling, as she does whenever an emergency vehicle passes by on the main road across from our home. I thought of getting the boys to go out on the balcony to watch the fire truck or ambulance rush by but decided not to interrupt their play time.

Ten minutes later, Jeff's partner knocked on the door. I opened the door and he looked white.

I just said, "Hi, what's happening?" as he had left our home when Jeff did.

He said, "Jeff has had a heart attack and I need to take you to the Austin Hospital."

For a moment I thought he must have been joking, but then I could tell by the look on his face that he was serious and that I needed to go. I told him I had to make some phone calls, so I ran in and rang my mum, Jeff's parents, Liam's friend's mum and then Jeff's heart specialist and they suggested to take in the drugs he was on for his heart complaint, atrial fibrillation.

I felt as though I was in overdrive and just going through the motions. I don't think I could fully appreciate the enormity of the reality, and it didn't make any sense to me why Peter was here telling me about the situation since I thought the police would have been here to do that, so I wasn't fully absorbing the severity of what I was about to confront. So then Peter drove me to the Austin Hospital. I asked why and how he came to find out about what had happened. He said that the Police had found Jeff's business card and rang Peter's number from that. He kept saying that he'd be okay but that it was very serious. I think he was in shock and perhaps denial too.

We arrived at Austin Hospital and they took me straight into casualty to see Jeff. On the way through I saw that his brother Ron, and parents were already there. I remember a small unusual looking doctor just look at me with an expression of hopelessness. Jeff was lying there on the hospital bed with plugs all over him, and breathing with a tube down his throat. All I could say to him was that I needed him. I begged him not to leave me, but I felt like I was watching a scene on TV and couldn't really take it all in. It's difficult to explain how I was feeling, but I felt so terribly alone and hopeless. I remember thinking that they weren't doing enough; they weren't rushing to do anything. It just didn't seem right to me. His mother and father came in, and his brother and his father started wailing, which I found very difficult to take.

A counsellor came to see me, and she suggested that we

look together at what details we had been told and then work through them. I felt like she was wasting my time and not really helping me in any way, as she had nothing new to inform me about the situation.

They decided to move Jeff over to the Warringal Private Hospital by ambulance, and suggested that I travel with him. I remember that they were breathing for him by just squeezing air into his mouth, and I didn't think they were doing it correctly or worrying about timing; it just didn't seem right to my way of thinking. There were two lovely women that were from the Diamond Creek ambulance that had been at the scene where he had collapsed, and they spoke to me about what had actually happened. They reassured me that everything was being done that could be.

Once settled in Warringal, a female doctor said to me that I had to decide whether I wanted my husband in a nursing home for the rest of his life or to let him go. I thought it was way too soon to be making that sort of decision, but I don't remember being really shocked by the statement. I think I just thought she was giving me the worst-case scenario. Jeff's heart specialist came in to see him, and I spoke with him. He gave me a more positive feeling, but I think underneath it all, I felt very hopeless.

The nursing staff suggested it was a good idea for the kids to come in and see Jeff straight away, which surprised me, and said that they could answer any of their questions. This was really important for them. I remember asking Ron to keep his father away from the kids if he were to continue wailing uncontrollably; it was upsetting enough without seeing and hearing him, and it was getting to me. I also found it very hard as Ron's wife and two children were there the whole time, including at the doctors' meetings, but I didn't feel as though I could say anything, as Jeff was their family too. I found this really hard, and felt so alone in dealing with all these issues. I felt as though I just had to go along with whatever was happening.

They chilled Jeff to help stop further brain damage. He normally loved being cool, but it was awful that he felt so cold, so unlike him. He looked so well and as though he was going to wake up at any moment. The nursing staff had that same look on their faces as the doctor at the Austin, and I felt hopeless.

I was also eight months pregnant.

Jeff was transferred back to the Austin on the Friday night as they had better equipment over there to cover the weekend, and they wanted to do as many tests as possible to make the correct diagnosis. I remember Ron greeting me one morning and saying that Jeff's kidneys were working better, but I just couldn't muster the same hope as he had.

I stayed at Mum and Dad's house over the week. I would get up in the morning and come home to shower and organise messages on the phone, the mail, our clothing and then go back to Mum's and either Mum or Dad would drive me back to the hospital. Each morning over breakfast with Mum and Dad I would just cry, then go home to shower. I remember feeling as though my crying wasn't strong enough to match the way I felt; I just felt so empty and alone. The kids would still be asleep or just waking when I got back so they would see me okay and then Mum usually would bring them into the hospital at some stage during the day.

On the Tuesday morning we had a meeting at the hospital with the doctors and my worst fears were realised: Jeff was dying. When he had the cardiac arrest his brain was starved of oxygen for about an hour. All the tests were showing nothing positive and that his major organs were deteriorating.

On Wednesday we spent most of the day by his side. His condition was worsening and it was becoming more and more upsetting seeing him like this. At 6pm I decided that he would want me to have tea with the kids, as they were his whole life, and I think it was important for me to spend time with them as well.

The intensive care staff gave me a beeper so they could contact me if they needed to, so we went down to the cafeteria. It was being renovated and I remember going through a sliding door to the outside and then into the temporary building where the cafeteria was. The wind was wild and eerie.

We all got our meals and we sat: Mum, Sarah, Liam, Jeff's mum and aunty, and my sister, Susie. We began having crazy conversations about anything and everything and we were laughing as we were recalling some thing or other when all of a sudden the beeper went off. For a split second, we all just looked at each other in silence. Fearing the worst, we raced back up to his room.

It seemed to take forever to get back there. There were doctors and nurses in the room and I pushed them aside and threw myself into Jeff's arms, moving them around me to be as close as I could to him as I possibly could.

He passed away as I held him.

People say that the deceased look so peaceful after dying; I was aware of nothing peaceful at all. I just thought it was awful and so not fair. I decided that the hospital chaplin could let the kids know that their father had passed away, which I hope was the right decision because I couldn't really function and felt removed from the whole situation.

I said to Jeff's mum that I wanted the two of us to be the last people to be with Jeff. My niece was running around the hospital crazed, my sister-in-law having to retrieve her from intensive care. Jeff's mum and I went back in to be with Jeff; to be with my husband, for the last time.

When we were leaving the hospital and walking over the footbridge, I noticed that the wind had died down, and it just felt peaceful. Ron let off a balloon from the bridge. I felt so hollow and helpless.

My life as I knew it had just ended.

The funeral parlour people came around to my parents' home after lunch, as well as all Jeff's family and his business partner. We made all the arrangements together, but it just didn't seem to be real. I wasn't in the moment, and it is a very difficult experience to describe. As Jeff was a fire fighter, his business partner suggested the funeral be held at Ivanhoe Town Hall, but I wanted it to be at the church where we were married, right across the road from our home. It was also just near where Jeff had collapsed the week before.

On Friday, Mum took me to my appointment in Richmond with my renal specialist and then I asked her if we could go home via the Victoria Market, so I could pick up some jam donuts, the way Jeff and I always had. Jeff and the kids and I would often call in to pick up jam donuts, and the then head off to the South Melbourne Market to pick up some South Melbourne dim sims on the weekend. It felt strange and very sad, with no Jeff there with me.

At 1am on the Saturday morning my waters broke. I woke Mum and before long we were on the way to Frances Perry House. Claire Charlotte Newland was born at 9am by caesarean section. It was so strange to feel so distraught and yet know that I should be happy with the arrival of my new baby. I believe Jeff had a hand in her early arrival, as I don't think it could have been timed any better. It gave everyone something else to think about other than the obvious, and I could get away from everything to contemplate Jeff's funeral and my life ahead.

It was hectic in the hospital with people dropping in all throughout visiting hours and nurses trying to control this without much luck. I organised the funeral with the help of Ron, my sister Susie and my girlfriends Kellie and Tracey. I knew I wanted it to be a celebration of Jeff's life, remembering the good times we had had with him in our life, rather than it being a sad, sad day.

I didn't know how I was going to attend the funeral. I was feeling so crushed, and I felt like I wouldn't be able to handle it but knew I had to. My obstetrician was great and allowed me to take Claire with me for the day, but it was on the condition that I come back to the hospital afterwards and stay until Friday. They organised for me to attend in a wheelchair because of the caesarean section. Dad picked us up from the hospital and we drove to their home and I sat with the kids while we all got ready to go.

We arrived at the church, and I said to Liam, "Look how famous your dad was!" There were around six hundred people there. The service was perfect, exactly how I wanted it, even giving me a laugh during some of the eulogies. Again, I felt like I was watching on and not actually participating in the moment. I really think Jeff somehow helped me through the service, and I even felt as though I could have spoken, which is so far from what I would ever have thought I would feel like. I didn't use the wheelchair as instructed.

The fire fighters formed a guard of honour down the main road outside the church, and I stood at the top of the road and looked down just feeling very awkward, very much alone, even though my family were beside me. There was no one there to lean on I guess.

The wake was held next door at a reception centre and was just a sea of people. I had to sit down and people continually came up to give me their condolences. I remember talking to ladies from my tennis team and raving on about something to do with tennis, and then feeling embarrassed afterward because it seemed such a trivial thing to talk about when I was at my husband's funeral. My sister insisted that I go into another room to breastfeed Claire, and it was so weird sitting in the quiet room with my baby; it was such a contrast. Claire was so good that day, not even crying when her feed was so late.

We went back to Mum and Dad's house after everyone had left, had a bite to eat, and then they took Claire and me back to the hospital. The quietness that night was deafening, but perhaps the hospital time was my saving grace. I could think alone and bond with my new baby.

Mum picked me up at about 10am on Friday morning and took me home. I knew I needed to go home then or maybe I never would. The kids were there to greet us, and my neighbour across the road came over to have a joke with me. It was really what we all needed.

LINDA

It was in the midst of joyous festive season celebrations that Linda and Rick's lives changed forever.

On the 26th December 2005, Rick and I were at home and in the middle of clearing Christmas leftovers when he had a major aneurism. He lived, but he was profoundly affected, and the next six months were enormously difficult. Three of those months were spent in intensive care for various reasons, complications and so forth. Eventually he was able to go to a rehabilitation hospital, but he was still unable to speak except for a few words. He was profoundly disabled. He had almost no mobility and was learning to recognize objects and feed himself.

Six months after all this happened, somehow or other, he was in a wheelchair, and he got out of the hospital, he went down the lift and got up onto the street outside the hospital and somehow tipped out of his wheelchair. He hit his head and this caused a bleed that was worse than the original one, and he died as a result of his injuries.

There are all sorts of issues with Rick's death to do with

who is responsible and what took place on the day and all that kind of stuff, and there really hasn't yet been any closure at all around the circumstances surrounding his death.

Because Rick was the person he was, in the public eye, Director of the National Farmers' Union, the outpouring of grief was just amazing. It wasn't a private death. Most of the Cabinet, and the Premier and former Prime Ministers attended his funeral. What happened with the ashes was another matter; that was very private.

ROSE

The changes in Andrew's demeanour were too subtle to alert Rose to the tragic twist in fate that awaited her family.

I watched Andrew begin to change. He was a wonderful father with the children, but things were becoming troubled between us. There was something not right about him. He seemed distant or depressed for some time. I didn't know anyone who had been depressed before, so I had little understanding of what was going on with him.

It began on the Saturday. He was staying with his mother at the time and he came over. I had guests coming over later for lunch and so had asked that he wait until later before coming over, but instead, he came around first thing. I was still getting things ready for the lunch and was surprised to see him. I was going to make pasta and get a French stick and a couple of other things.

I suggested he come for a walk with us to the bread shop where I could get the French stick and a few extra things to have with our lunch. He was behaving quite strangely; his energy was kind of hyper. What I didn't know was he had been to the doctor and told him that he needed some sleeping tablets, because we were having trouble in the marriage and he needed something to help him sleep at night. All these weeks he hadn't been sleeping. Anyway, we left to go to the bakery; I thought we could have a coffee together while we were out.

At a table behind us there was a little boy who had a very noticeable birthmark on his face. He was only very young, and Andrew began asking him about it and I thought it was very unlike him to be asking so many questions. He was clearly upsetting the boy and his parents. I was in quiet disbelief.

All of a sudden he started slurring and swaying, and he was dribbling, and I thought he was having a stroke. He said, "No I'm not, I just took a sleeping tablet." I said, "You took a sleeping tablet now? You're supposed to take those things before you go to bed!" Then he said he had taken six. I said to the lady I knew who worked there that I had to go home to get the car to take him to the doctor.

Of all things, there was a nurse at the next table. By the time I got back with the car, the nurse said that he had revealed to her that he had taken the whole bottle. So she followed me with her car to the doctor's surgery, and luckily the doctor was there. The doctor kept talking to Andrew attempting to keep him awake. He said, "I'll phone the emergency department and tell them you're on your way."

When we got to the hospital, they charcoaled his stomach

or whatever it is that they do, and when they were done, they told me he was okay and that he could go home.

I was going to take him back home and look after him there, but for some reason, something made me think of the children. I was worried for them. So I took him home to his mum so she could look after him that night.

The next morning, I went to pick him up because we had an appointment at the real estate agents' that I hadn't been able to change. I thought it would be good for him to be out and about, to lift his spirits a bit after what had happened yesterday. And so I went there at about 11am, and he was sitting on the couch in the lounge room and he looked different; grey, removed. He had on his pyjamas and his robe, and I asked him why he wasn't dressed yet, because we were supposed to get to the appointment, and then I had to go and pick up the kids from school, so we only had a certain amount of time. I was trying to get him up and dressed.

I'll never forget his face. He got up very slowly and walked out of the room. I thought he was getting dressed. And I was talking with his mother, asking her how he was doing. He seemed all right, you know? Next thing, he went into his own room, locked the door and pulled the blind down.

Andrew shot himself that morning. Even in recalling all of this now, there is such a heavy silence in the midst of this picture in my mind, just like viewing a film on mute, without the volume turned on. I can still see myself running outside in terror and calling the authorities for help on my mobile. The paramedics arrived before the police did, and my understanding is that they are supposed to wait until the police get there before they do anything, but time was running out and they had to kick the door down so as to be able to get to him. Before they did this, we were asked to wait outside. Andrew was rushed to casualty by ambulance and we followed by police escort.

He was in there for what seemed the longest time. They came back to us at 2pm. I remember looking at the head nurse who was in charge of that whole area, and thinking, "Uh oh, this is not good. I have a bad feeling about this." She just looked at me.

And then the doctor came down. He still had his cap on, and he was removing gloves or something from his hands, and he looked at me, and he couldn't even speak. He was trying not to cry, and he took my hands, and then I remember I held his, and I said, "It's okay. He didn't make it, did he?" And he just shook his head.

Everyone was just beside themselves with grief. Somehow I managed to find the strength to be able to help everyone else in the room. I believed it was important for me to contain myself, as this would help the others to deal with the shocking announcement. I then faced the gruesome task of telling Andrew's mother that he had died.

There's a viewing room, in the hospital, where you see the body before they take it away. The nurse was going to take me down to see him but they needed to clean him up first. I remember looking at him and then all of a sudden recalling a dream that I had had sometime ago. I dreamt that I'd seen him lying there, like this. And there he was. And I was looking at him, in this room, a viewing room. It was all very surreal. It was like time was standing still.

I walked up to where he lay. I gently touched his cheek. He was still warm. I stroked his soft, dark hair and I said to him, "You sausage! You silly sausage! What were you thinking?"

To think that, just like that, his life was over! Just like that! This morning we were talking with each other in the lounge room. And now he was here in the hospital, in a viewing room. The man I had married lay in a viewing room in front of me! By this time, I felt numb. It was a sinking feeling, heavy, odd. I had to get out of there. I had to get away from that place.

We left the hospital soon after and went home. I arranged to have someone pick up the children from school. I was in shock; I was numb and in a state of disbelief.

The blaming began right away. There were certain relatives who believed I was responsible for what had happened. Fortunately however, we had a huge network of family and friends who were there to offer support during this time.

In the days after his death, there was this great procession of people through the house. The visits were brief, but many, because of the number of people dropping by. It went on for days, getting to the point that, after the funeral, we had to eat out most nights just to get away and create space for ourselves. We did this for some time, but everything settled down after awhile.

You know, suicide has such a stigma to it. It can be very confusing for everyone involved. You are left with so many unanswered questions, and these questions haunted me for many months after Andrew died.

Cancer affects one in three men and one in four women in Australia before the age of seventy-five. For the patients and family of those who confront such a diagnosis, the preciousness of each day is paramount.

David has been gone for seven years now, and he was diagnosed seven years previously. He had prostate cancer. The surgeons and he decided that he needed to have the operation, and get rid of it, which they managed to. He had to have chemo and radiation treatment and he always used to say that was worse than the actual complaint he had, and he used to feel very sick afterwards.

He went into remission, and that was great. But It came back. And It came back with a vengeance. He went back and had his check up and they said it had come back again, and they said he only had six months to live. He lasted seven.

They were unable to operate. It had gone too far. I didn't believe it. And he didn't want to go in and have the treatment again, because that used to make him really, really sick. And there was nothing else they could do for him. That was it; they'd done all that they could do.

I didn't believe that this was true; I didn't believe it was going to happen. I'm not quite sure about what David thought because he kept his feelings to himself. When he found out he had it, he wanted life to go on as usual and he didn't want to change anything, so he went and sang in his chorus, and I would go to tap dancing lessons, and we were involved in the theatre, and our kids, and that was it. Of course, there were days when he felt sick and he had to go to bed, but apart from that we tried to live our lives as normally as possible.

Looking back, I don't know whether that was such a good thing. Maybe that was one way of not dealing with it, you know? If everything is normal, then everything is going to be all right. Or that may have been the only way he could deal with it, I don't know. I have no idea how I would feel if somebody said to me that I only had six months to live. How does one cope with that? I wouldn't know.

David had such a wonderful personality; he never gave up. He had rheumatoid arthritis and psoriasis, and when he used to do *The Follies* he would spend four days in bed after they had finished because he hurt so much. And I'd ask him why he did it, if it caused him so much pain, but he'd insist that it was worth it because he got so much enjoyment out of it.

When he was told he only had six months, we were right in the middle of rehearsing for *The Follies*. Eventually he had to give it away of course, because he was too sick. But I kept rehearsing. If he felt okay he would come down to rehearsals with me and watch. If he didn't of course he would just stay at home and I would go down, do my bit, and then come home again. I think I have photos somewhere of him at that time, up on stage singing, rehearsing for *The Follies*. Somebody had taken photos.

He passed away while *The Follies* were on.

I was only doing the chorus stuff, so it didn't matter if I backed out. One person missing was not going to make that much difference. I had no plans to do any sketches because I knew that if anything did happen, I would have to back out, which I did of course. I had to. I think I performed for one week, and then I had to give it away.

He was cremated on the Saturday, and it was the last night of the show that night, and we asked if we could use the hall, which they allowed us to do, and we decorated it. I put hundreds of balloons in there, because I'm a balloon person, I just love balloons! They also left one of the sketches from the show up on the stage in David's honour. It looked great. The whole hall looked great.

But I performed that night. I actually went and performed on the Saturday night. We had the service there in the morning, we went and had him cremated, and that night, I went and performed with the theatre company.

I suppose I performed that night was because I didn't believe that he'd really gone! I was quite literally in a state of disbelief. It was like he was still around, that he was still in hospital and he'd be out in two or three weeks. It was a total denial that he had gone. We'd had the service, we'd had the cremation, and we went back to Jody's and had people there for the wake. But it wasn't real. It was like it was for somebody else, not me! Not my David! Not us! This is not for me, this is for somebody else! It just wasn't real.

Now I think of it, I can't believe I actually went and performed! "You have just cremated your husband, your partner, your best friend, your buddy!" But at that time, in that moment, it was different. He always used to say, "The show must go on!" I'm sure he would have wanted it to, so in some ways I suppose I did it for him. And when we sang that night, the theatre company sang *The Entertainer* for David, because he loved that song so much.

I think in reality if I'd sat back and thought, "Oh my god, this is really going to happen," I think I would have been a different person. The way I dealt with it was the best way for me at that time. And it was possibly the best way to make David's life as happy as possible until the end, because that's what we did; we just did whatever he wanted. I think going to work helped me deal with it too. David and I discussed that. I said I'd give up work, and he said, "What for? I sleep. I can still get up and make myself a drink, a sandwich. What are you going to do? Sit there and watch me sleep?" And so I went to work. At the time it seemed the right thing to do. Now when I look back, however, I very much doubt that it was the right thing to do. Maybe I should have stayed at home.

I never knew he was going to go when he did go. As far as we were concerned, they were trying new treatment, trying to get his medication right and trying to get everything on an even keel. But it just wasn't going to happen, was it?

He woke up on Thursday night and said, "I've got pain."

And I said, "Where have you got pain?"

"In my back"

And I asked him, "Do you want me to drive you to hospital?"

He told me in no uncertain terms, "No, I don't like your driving, you're too jittery. Ring up Paul and get him to drive me in."

So Paul drove us in.

They didn't have a bed for him so he had to stay in the

74

emergency department, in the room there, and they gave him morphine for the pain so he was zonked out. I took Paul back home because he had to go to work in the morning. And David didn't even know that I'd left and come back. They found him a bed at 2pm in the afternoon and took him up to the ward and that's when they tried to stabilise him, to get his medication right and all that sort of thing.

And then, on the following Monday, a friend of mine who lives nearby woke up and said to his wife, "I think I might go in and see David today." So he went in. And Jody went in. Neal went in, Jody's husband. And the three of the men from the quartet went in. And so the four of them, with David, went around to all the wards and sang to everybody! And then I went in. Paul came in a bit later. And some of the people from the Theatre Company also came in. This was all on the Monday.

He had a magical day. We were lying on his bed together, singing an African song from *The Follies*.

David asked, "How does that African song go?" and he started singing it.

And I was lying on the bed saying, "No! No! No! It doesn't go like that!" I can't remember it now of course.

And Paul was still sitting there and he said, "However it goes, it sounds terrible!"

And then we left at about half past ten that night.

On the Tuesday morning he was supposed to go down and have some new treatment, and they came in for him.

He said to the nurse, "I really don't feel like going for it yet, I really don't feel great."

The nurse said to him, "That's okay, we'll do it later."

And he just sat back and closed his eyes, and that was it.

They phoned me at work that morning and said that he had passed away.

I said, "That can't be!"

He had said to me on the Monday night, "I've had such a magical day! It's been so good! I've had such a great day!"

And so when they rang me and told me this, it was just total, total disbelief. I could not believe that it happened because he had had such a great day, and he was on a high, he felt so good. It didn't make any sense, how could this be?

If you ask me if I remember any of that day I don't. I drove to the hospital, but I don't remember driving there. In fact, when I saw him I thought he was going to wake up at any minute because that's what he looked like, he looked asleep, as peaceful as anything.

Paul and Jody were there, and his nephew, and a few other people.

It was sheer disbelief. He was in a two-bed ward, and he'd only been in there since Thursday and then he passed away on the Tuesday! The woman from the other ward came down the corridor and got hold of me and cuddled me and she was sobbing!

She said, "I just cannot believe it! I cannot believe it! I am so, so sorry!"

It's not real; it's as though you're dreaming and any minute you're going to wake up, and everything's going to be okay. It's so hard to describe to anybody how you feel because it's confusing enough for yourself. It's as though you're in another world. Nothing is real!

You think, "When I wake up, he's going to be there, and it's all going to be okay!"

I believed he was going to walk through that door for a long time after he had gone. I didn't accept his passing away, and I think that was because he was having such a great day on the Monday that it was inconceivable to me that he had gone. It was unbelievable that he could have been there, looking so good, having such a great time, and then the next day, not be there at all.

There are stages that you go through with cancer, and you prepare yourself for them, and you think that there is maybe a month or two or three months of going though this stage, and then one moves on to the next stage, and so it's a gradual process. And I think this way you learn to cope with the cancer better, rather than have it happen the way it happened for us. It was so sudden. Those stages you anticipate were ripped away from us.

Once David had got to palliative care, I would have given up work, and stayed at home of course. So then I felt guilty, because I hadn't given up work. And then I'd thought I should have given up work and stayed at home to be with him and not listened to what he said. So I felt extremely guilty about not having been there. How could I have let him be that sick and not be at home? But then I probably still wouldn't have been there because I would have been at home and he would have been at the hospital anyway if it had have happened on the same day, so I don't know. There are lots of ifs, whys and what fors.

I think it was wonderful for David that he didn't have

to go through further suffering. Jody said to me later that she and Paul had been walking down the hospital corridor one day (David was at the far end of it.) Along it there were single rooms where terminal patients went when they were near the end. These patients more or less had morphine pumped into them so they wouldn't feel any pain. Jody said, "Paul and I were talking about Dad being managed like that and we were just dreading the prospect of his getting to that stage."

Well he never ever got to that stage. But I wasn't dreading that because at least he'd still be here! Albeit not remembering very much, or not really knowing whether I'd be there or not, but he'd be there and he'd be alive. But on the other hand, I suppose it's not good for the person even if they don't really know very much about it. That's no life; it's certainly no quality of life.

It is funny how you look at life isn't it?

I always said, "Don't let me linger!"

I wouldn't want to linger! I wouldn't want to be a burden. And yet when you are faced with that situation, you would do anything to keep that person alive. On the other hand, how David went was magic, for him. When you think about it, I don't think that he could have gone on a better day, because on the Monday he had had such a wonderful day.

ELWYN

For Elwyn and Cathy, cancer would also determine the future of their lives together. The initial prognosis seemed hopeful.

Cathy discovered a lump under her left arm, and a biopsy confirmed it to be bone cancer. We were given two options: lose the whole arm, or remove the piece of bone from the shoulder to the elbow, and replace it with one of her collarbones. We took the second option and saved her arm. Cathy then had chemotherapy, losing her beautiful long blonde hair in the process.

We thought things were all right, however a routine scan a year later showed tumours growing in both her lungs. Two more operations and more chemotherapy resulted in the loss of her hair again. A year later she got a tumour in her leg and it was discovered that the tumours were back in both lungs again. Three operations later and whole lobes of her lungs removed made it difficult for her to breathe.

Just prior to Cathy's routine check, she noticed a few small tumours appearing on her leg and back. We now anticipated even more operations and chemotherapy. The scans showed that the tumours were out of control, and were all over her body. The oncologist told us there was nothing more they could do and we only had a matter of weeks.

Cathy was relieved it was over as she didn't want any more operations or chemotherapy. We were given prescriptions of morphine and told the pain would soon become unbearable. I immediately took time off work to look after Cathy, as it was now becoming more difficult for her to breathe. If I was facing her at night, or the heating came on, she would wake up with a slight drop in the oxygen level. It was too cold to open the windows, so we decided to go to Queensland.

It was the September school holidays so the kids came

with us. Cathy was now in a wheelchair and was on regular oxygen. We were at Burleigh Heads on the Gold Coast staying in a room, which overlooked a swimming pool and spa. Then, on one particular day, Cathy decided that she wanted to go into the pool, and so that's what we did. Later that evening we were sitting on the balcony overlooking the beach, and she said that she had had a wonderful day and that Burleigh Heads was such a beautiful place.

Soon afterwards, we noticed that Cathy was starting to lose consciousness, so we called an ambulance that took her to the hospital. They told us there was nothing they could do, and she didn't have long to go. She had no energy to talk, and tried to write but failed. She finally had the strength to whisper that she wanted to get out of there and not die in a hospital. We called her brother David in Brisbane who came back to the motel with us.

Cathy knew it would be her last day, and insisted that we all drag our mattresses into the family room and all sleep together. She needed permanent oxygen to help her breathe, and that made her throat dry. Everything she tried to eat and drink went straight into her lungs and made her cough. She said we were so lucky to be able to drink because she wasn't able to.

By this time, Cathy was falling in and out of consciousness and when she stopped breathing I panicked and told David to ring triple zero. I quickly laid her down and started breathing into her mouth and she coughed and spluttered and started breathing again. I told my son to turn up the oxygen to 6%, but before long Cathy took her last breath as I held her in my arms.

The emergency operator asked if I wanted to start CPR, but I had to make the painful decision not to, as her poor body just didn't have the energy to fight for another breath.

It was 3.15am on Monday 29th September 2003.

I had to try and be strong and not show too much emotion because my three kids were distraught. David took the kids out of the room for me because I didn't want them to see their mum being put into a body bag.

It was absolutely horrible coming back to Melbourne without her.

PAUL S

Paul did not see that his wife, Delina's weight loss as anything unusual as she had always taken great care to keep herself slim.

All throughout our married life Delina was very weight conscious. She was a beautiful size fourteen when we met. To me that was not overweight but she began dieting over the years, and with her persistence she got down to a size ten. I used to tell her that she had become anorexic and to put some weight back on.

In 2006 Delina was steadily going off food and lost a huge amount of weight. I argued with her to try and get her to eat more food and she tried to just to keep me happy.

The alarm bells still did not ring for me until just before her diagnosis with cancer. I noticed a lump on her abdomen that she had been hiding from me obviously for quite some time. She was worried about the lump but had a real fear of doctors.

I finally talked her into seeing a doctor and she had some tests done. On the July 25th 2006, Delina had a doctor's appointment to get the test results. She was at work and was going to see her doctor straight after work. That morning the doctor rang me at home and asked me to be with Delina as she wanted to discuss her test results with both of us. I immediately feared the worst.

We were both told together by her doctor that Delina had cancer in the liver and that it was too late do much about it. I immediately broke down. Delina however, possibly through shock, took it almost jokingly. We were told that the only option available to her was chemotherapy but not as a cure, only to prolong her life. The more the doctor told us, the more I wailed. Poor Delina was not only trying to cope with the terrible news, but she was also trying to console me.

Delina was admitted to hospital and was in her ward within two hours of being told the terrible news. I was with Delina for a while but had to keep going outside her room as I kept breaking down. I tried not to let her see me crying so as not to upset her.

Delina was given three months to live. She lived for three months and sixteen days. There was a steady decline in her health and emotional state. She had five doses of chemotherapy and two sessions of radiotherapy in those three months, never really regaining any of her strength between doses.

During those three months, Delina was home for some of the time. The last time she was admitted before her passing, I had to call an ambulance. She was in the back of the ambulance with the paramedics. I was standing in the driveway. We looked at each other and I wondered to myself whether she would ever see our house again.

Delina never came back home. The last three weeks of her life I was with her constantly, to the point that the nursing staff were telling me to go home and to get some rest. I refused to leave. I wanted to spend as much time as possible with Delina. Our time together was coming to an end.

The night before Delina passed away I could sense that death was close. I asked the nursing staff if I could stay with her that night and they agreed. Delina was transferred to a single room and they supplied me with a folding bed, which I did not use, preferring instead to sit with her all night.

Delina saw that night through. Her breakfast arrived which she did not look at or touch. Yet another blood test was done that morning. Her arms were black and blue from the bruising from all the blood tests she was given. I remember begging with the doctor to give Delina a blood transfusion as her blood was not recovering from each dose of chemo.

He replied, "There is no need for that."

I find it very difficult to think about Delina's final moments.

The oncologist's registrar came to see Delina just a few minutes after 11am. She examined her and motioned to me to go outside Delina's room with her. She said to me that she wanted permission to stop all Delina's medication. I was astounded by her request.

I replied, "No, definitely not!"

I asked why she wanted to do this. The doctor explained that Delina was on the strongest possible medication, that nothing was working and that I should "let her slip away." This sounded so cold and callous to me. I became angry. I had never heard of such a thing.

I asked how long my wife could last without medication and was told one or two days.

I replied, "But she probably only has two days left with medication! You definitely cannot withdraw her medication!" and walked back into Delina's room. I am sure that Delina heard what was taking place outside her room.

I sat with my wife once again and held her hand. Delina opened her eyes and ever so gently squeezed my hand with all the strength she could muster. She looked me in the eyes and gave me the most beautiful smile I have ever seen in my life, a smile I will cherish for as long as I live.

At 11.10am that morning, Delina passed away.

When she passed away, I thought she had just fainted. I ran out of her room into the passageway, yelling for help. A number of nurses quickly rushed in but just stood at her bedside doing nothing. I yelled at them to do something but they told me it was too late, that she had gone.

I became hysterical. I leaned over and hugged and kissed my beautiful wife's lifeless body. I tried to do CPR but one of the nurses pulled me away.

My beautiful Delina had left me.

After I had calmed down a bit, they left me alone with my wife and closed the door. I told her I felt that her spirit was in the room with me. I was crying uncontrollably.

Delina passed away on the 9th November 2006. It was one day after our 31st wedding anniversary.

ERIKA

During a visit to Canberra Erika's life changed suddenly and without warning.

Damian was away in Canberra for work. The boys and I had decided to come along and spend some time at a music festival that was on. Damian and I made plans for meeting up later at an event in the evening.

He collapsed and died at work just before the start of the course he was preparing. I got news that he had collapsed and went to the hospital, not thinking that it would be serious. Maybe a migraine.

Driving along the highway, I remember thinking about how I could convince him to take the day off, rather than going straight back to the course as soon as he felt a bit better. I thought how nice it would be if this meant he would not teach the course and we could spend time together instead.

I remember everything at the hospital. The room. The sounds. The touch of the nurse. Words. Damian. The realisation. The priest. A call to my parents. A friend. Damian's aunts. Cousins. My boys arriving. The words. The scream. The room. Damian. The police. The room. Damian. My boy.

Damian.

ANN

A simple day away from work became a living nightmare.

I was off work with a cold. As a prison warden, you are working twelve-hour shifts, so it wasn't like an office job where you could go and then get to sort of 2pm and say, "I've had enough; I'm going to go home." You had to be basically up to it, for fourteen hours, from leaving in the morning to getting home that night. So anyway, I was in bed with Patrick. He wasn't rostered on that day. He was going into town to get his medals done up properly, and then he was going to do something else while he was in town. It was a bit of a last minute thing, and he asked me to come along for the ride, but I didn't feel up to it. I wanted to stay in bed.

He said to me, "When I get back I'll make a chicken curry, and I'll put the recycling out and…"

I've never been able to remember what the third thing was. And that was about ten o'clock in the morning.

I was in the shower about an hour later and I remember getting out of the shower and thinking, "Oh damn! I forgot to wash my hair!" I wasn't really there. It wasn't like one of those days where it didn't matter; it mattered, it was revolting. And I was just starting to put my clothes on when the phone rang. It was a Sergeant Downs. I don't remember the particular conversation but the gist of it was that Patrick was in emergency at St. Vincent's. He'd had a fall. A fall? What's a fall? Sort of like tripped over the edge of the pavement and got hit by a car? A fall? What's a fall? A fall didn't make sense. My first thought was that Patrick had lost his cool! What's he done? I thought he'd been arrested or something because he'd lost his temper or something and I was freaking out. Little did I know.

The policeman sounded like he was out of his depth. He didn't know what to say to me. And he put the doctor on and the doctor said, "He's had a massive heart attack and we don't expect him to survive."

It took a moment for me to comprehend what had just been said. I'd always had this thing, this belief, about us, about Patrick. So I was thinking, "He's never going to die without me! He can't die! He'll hang on! They don't know Patrick! They don't know us!" Yeah right. That went out the window quick smart. They wanted me there urgently.

I went up to Mum and Dad's house. They had initially taken the call. The police couldn't trace me because I have a silent number. Mum and Dad's phone number was the only number they had for that address which would have been on Patrick's licence, so they didn't actually get through to me at first, so dad knew there was something wrong anyway. And then we had to drive into the hospital. It was bizarre.

Dad kept saying, "Slow down! Slow down! There's no point if you're dead as well! You won't get there any faster!"

It was the slowest twenty-five minutes of my life!

I remember driving along near where the hospital is, and if you come up Gisborne Street I think, where the Fire Museum is, and you turn right and if you miss that little road, it's very hard to get back.

And so I had to just pull up and say, "Dad, park the car!"

I jumped out and then tried to run, and all I can remember

is that my legs were like lead. I didn't feel like I could move.

And I got in there and was taken into a little room where it's all quiet, and they explained to me what exactly lay ahead trying to prepare me. I was thinking, "Why have you taken me into this room? Do you think I don't know how bad it is going to look?"

My brother Ian arrived at the same time. We went in together. Patrick was on a ventilator, and they'd cut all his clothes off, and they were carrying on and they had the cardiologist and the this and the that, and at one point it was pretty horrible because he'd started doing that convulsing thing that people do when they've had a stroke. And he was grimacing as though he was crying.

And I heard, "That's just a reflex!"

And all I really wanted to say, "What a fucking bitch! What do you, mean, it's just a reflex!"

I mean, I don't know if it was a reflex or not, as far as I was concerned it was pain and suffering. I just interpreted it as his wanting to talk to me and he couldn't. They say some of the stupidest things! They put him into ICU (Intensive Care Unit) and I stayed there that night. One of my friends came in and stayed for a while. And she kept on getting me cups of tea with sugar in it. I don't even have tea with sugar but she insisted that I had to have some sugar.

And I remember walking through into the Intensive Care Unit saying, "I'm too young to be a widow! I'm forty-two, I'm too young to be a widow!"

They have pastoral care at the hospital. And there was an awful woman, and she was being sort of 'jolly' towards me.

And she gave me this big hug, and I remember thinking, "Get your body off me!" Whatever she felt, she had nothing to do with me! I didn't need this woman to clutch me and somehow think that she was supporting me! To me, she was supporting herself!

And so I stayed there that night, and the sound of the monitors was awful. Every now and then the respirators would go down, and then Patrick would make these noises, and I'd think that he was he's dying, and then it would pick up again. It was dreadful.

At one stage, this male nurse very unhelpfully came out with the statement, "Well if he'd survived, you know, he really wouldn't be able to do anything anyway; like he wouldn't be able to cross the room without help!"

"It's such a mess with a heart attack," he went on to tell me, "So much muscle has died, and he wouldn't be able to walk across the room without having to stop and rest". It was 2am, and I told him that that was more than enough information right now.

I was really blunt and direct with the nursing staff because of their attitude towards me which seemed to be "This is how we're going to do it" under the guise of "We're caring for you here as well you know."

And it wasn't so much that they weren't caring as that they had it in their head that there was a process, and that I had to step into line because that was what I was supposed to do. There was an assumption that because they have the knowledge, they'll tell you therefore what's going to happen, and you have no choice but to go along with it.

And I remember saying to one of them that I wanted this one thing. It was the Saturday night, the second night, and although it kind of doesn't make sense now, I insisted that they leave the respirator on overnight because at the time, I thought, I have to wake up one morning with the awareness of his still being alive, before I let him go. I just can't wake up and find that it's over. I have to have that waking up, that one moment where there's that millisecond when the world is okay, before your consciousness expands and you realise that it's not.

And I remember saying, "I have to have a night like that, I have to have a night and to be able to wake up and to be able to have that realisation and have him still here! You can't take him away before I've had that!" After all, what it meant to them was neither here nor there, it was nothing to them. But it was so important to me. I remember being really clear, saying to them, "Look your job is to look after him; my job is to look after me. So you do what you do, and I'm going to tell you what I need, so please don't make any decisions on my behalf. And don't you think you know what's best for me, because you don't. I need to do what I need to do so I can get through this, so I can get through these days."

And to this day I believe that Patrick hung on for me. They took him off the respirator at about 7am on Sunday morning so that's about forty-two hours after the heart attack. I stayed with Patrick Friday night and then stayed at my brother's on Saturday night and the Sunday night and then the Monday I stayed with Patrick again and so when I came back, they had taken the respirator off (without consulting me I might add) and they'd taken him up to the palliative care floor which is on the eleventh floor. It was nice up there, and the pastoral care worker there was just spot on, just perfect; Patrick would have liked her. So I was just coming back to him, and they had expected him to just die in the afternoon, but he actually didn't die for fifty-three hours after the respirator was removed. And I thought, "Yeah this is so Patrick! You guys have no idea who you've got here in this bed!"

So I needed those few days. He died four days after the heart attack, within an hour or two, and I really needed those four days.

The strange thing was that on the one level I knew he had had all his struggles with things like the PTSD but on another level, he had this quality about him that was invincible, and he was just so strong. So that's probably what was so shocking, because on one level it seemed possible, but on another level it was completely unbelievable.

On that last night, I think the nursing staff thought that perhaps it might be the last night, Monday night, I needed desperately to find a Buddhist because Patrick had become affiliated with Buddhism in Vietnam. He used to wear this little piece of leather around his foot and according to the Vietnamese Buddhists, this guaranteed that your spirit didn't get lost when it passed over. And I was panicking that the piece of leather was lost, and that his spirit would get lost, but then I found it; it was there, around his ankle.

And so I desperately wanted to find someone who could help him pass over. Toni, the pastoral care woman, was going to find someone who could come and do what Buddhists do when someone is dying, whatever that is, I don't know! Toni said there was someone who was a practising Buddhist who was a nurse at St. Vincent's, who happened to be working there that night. I can't remember the nurse's name, but I remember what he looks like, because I've seen him at a couple of Buddhist things since then. He looked a bit like Flacco. He had one shoulder a bit high and it seemed to be a bit uncomfortable. He came in wearing a beret, and he taught me a practice which was about breathing in the karma of the dying person to help them to pass over.

So that's what I did.

There's a room, which had a jelly bed for people who have had strokes, kind of soft and jelly-like so you avoid bedsores. And the nurses wheel you out in it, if they want to get you out of the room, and wheel you out onto the balcony or wherever. And so they put me into the jelly bed, and I just hung onto Patrick's hand, and then when they'd turn him over, they'd wheel me round to the other side and I'd just change hands. I did that all night.

And the nurse came and saw me at the end of his shift, in the morning. He was a really lovely person. And then when the other nurses looked at him when they arrived for the day shift, they checked around his ankles and at his feet, which were sort of going blue, and they said, "Yeah, he's going now." So it was as though he'd hung on for me, and then that was when he let go.

And Dad had brought CJ, Patrick's dog in one night to see him as well, to say goodbye. CJ had a bath before he came in and he was still hyper and jumped up and kissed Patrick and ran around and jumped up and kissed him again and had no idea of course.

The four of us were with him. Tony the pastoral care worker was there. And there were two of us on either side, holding his hands, mopping his brow. Rena my sister-in-law was there, and I was standing behind Patrick because I hate that look in their eyes, that 'looking but not there' look. When someone is clinically dead it's just really, really horrible.

After he died, I left the room while the nurses do what they do and when I came back, he was lying back straight, nose pointed to the ceiling, sheet pulled up to his chin, with a rose on his chest. I just freaked out, I absolutely freaked out. They were saying, "Oh, he's peaceful now, he looks peaceful now he's gone." I just collapsed and kept saying, "It's not him, it's not him!" It didn't look like him; it didn't feel like him. A corpse to me doesn't really look like a person anyway, somehow, the body doesn't look like the person, and there was something about his face that didn't look like Patrick at all.

I couldn't believe that Patrick had died. I couldn't believe that he had died and it was so quiet: there was no thunder, no fireworks, no mass yelling, no kind of noisy marking of his transition. A peaceful death is all very well spiritually, but emotionally, I wanted noise, lots of noise – anger, grief, a complaint, an expression of injustice. But all that greeted me was silence.

Leanne experienced increasingly persistent symptoms that eventually became too troubling to ignore.

In October 1999 Leanne began to complain of nausea, which we attributed to seasonal bugs going around. Leanne, being slow to investigate, thought little of it, and not fussing, soldiered on until other symptoms joined in at which point we had an X-ray done. Nothing showed. Pain symptoms persisted and worsened, steadily casting an ominous cloud over our little family.

Terribly worried in early 2000 with neck pain, continued weight loss, and finally that lump in her breast, I'd had enough of the fear. Not knowing, not having a diagnosis, to my mind was worse than knowing what was going on. We rang a specialist and had an appointment. X-rays were taken and we were sent home to wait.

Within the week we got a call from the specialist's office. I will never forget the silence of everything around us that morning as Leanne took the call. I was sweeping the kitchen floor; it was just another day. Leanne was concentrating on the voice on the other end of the phone. I remember her putting the phone down and falling back on the bed, then through a shaky voice telling me that the specialist urgently needs to see us at his office; there was no time to waste.

Everything went into a kind of shock fog after that. We knew it was bad, very bad. We called friends to stay with the kids, got a lift to the specialist, walked in, sat down, and prepared ourselves. He was very moved for the two of us. He produced the X-rays, put them up on the screen, and stepped back. He spoke softly to us, knowing what was slowly dawning and what a horrific assault it was for a family. The X-rays were a confirmation of what we had been hoping only happened to other people.

Now we were those people.

We were sent to the oncologist immediately, and after viewing the X-rays we were told that Leanne had a particularly aggressive form of carcinoma and that he would do his very best for us. We walked out into the world with our minds unable to function; we were on autopilot, bodies that work through habitual pattern training, but our minds had left the building.

Not long after diagnosis at a family meeting with the oncology team, our specialist informed us all that given the severity of Leanne's condition, we were looking at a life expectancy of between three and twelve months.

After the diagnosis, everything changed. These changes happened slowly at first: there were appointments, treatments, diet changes, new routines, family and friends coming and going, children aware of what was happening and watching their mum intently for any visible sign of her illness.

Leanne was caught in many a battle, not the least of these being over what treatment to follow, and what would give her the best possible chance. Should she try to find a way to pay for alternative treatments, or go with mainstream medicine? It seemed every minor thing associated with her life now had an attached rating. What impact would the choices she made, large or small, have on her life? Do I sleep now or later? When should I eat? Do I do this, or go there? Maybe if I take a new drug just released, then things may change and so on.

At this point, her life had become one of dependency. She took to the regimes of home style hospitalisation with all of it's privations with an oddly professional approach, setting up her own timetables and monitoring her medication and bodily functions as she would have in her nursing or mothering capacity, except now of course she was the patient.

She was allowed to self-administer small doses of morphine for pain. Oddly and thankfully, the pain was not as much of a problem as was fluid retention throughout her body. We thought that these small doses of morphine gave her a way to rise above the storm raging in and around her, as she and I were badly buffeted by the winds of change with the very visible sign of Leanne's worsening condition.

Not realising that I was in the grips of post traumatic stress disorder, I lost all reason and hope. The rage I felt at times was enormous. A lovely woman so committed to family and friends was to die. I doubt I could endure those times of suffering again. I felt it was a great injustice on the part of God.

Leanne begged me to look after our children. I made a promise to her that I would take care of them. On the night before she died, the kids came in to see Leanne and to have their last bedtime story with their mum.

On July 22nd 2000, at McCulloch House at the Monash Medical Centre, Leanne passed away. My sisters and brothers were there with me when she died.

4

Emptiness:
after they have gone

At the time of death, we are so caught up in the momentum
brought on by the chaotic business of funeral arrangements,
contacting people and sorting through belongings, that it may
not be until well after the wake that the full reality of the loss
sinks in.

When the guests have finally gone and we are left with
half-eaten sandwiches, dishes to wash and the hollow echoes of
an empty house for company, the emptiness and the significance
of our loss, begin to press heavily on our hearts.

Journal Entry

17th November 2002. White Dust and Ashes.

Stu.

I keep looking for you everywhere.

Along streets that used to be familiar; streets that used to be part of our little precious life together; our house in town, where we spent what seemed like so much time.

I remember the roar of a city that never slept; I remember the late, late nights when I would jump in a taxi at midnight and meet you at one of the many venues where you did your magic with music and lights; and I'd kiss little Jimmy goodnight and promise him Mum would be back soon.

But we weren't back of course until the wee hours when through a haze of smoke and alcohol we saw the sunrise, casting its rays of golden promise over a waking city.

Not so long ago, I returned to the streets of our old haunts.

I bit back the sting of tears as I realised yet again that that time had passed and what had been would never be again. Time is nothing if not transitory.

And then I quietly wept.

I was standing on the very same bridge overlooking the city skyline against a beautiful wintry sky that I used to stand upon and look out over the city with my Jimmy, our little pound puppy that you insisted one time we bring home to live with us. I could sense that time as though it were just yesterday; same worn asphalt under my feet, same bridge upon which I stood, same view from where I looked.

And yet so much was different.

I had tried to rebuild my life, bit by broken bit after everything that happened. And as I stood on this bridge, I wept not just at the passing of time, but at how much we still loved each other, such was our love, and the long years we had spent together.

Yesterday I had to return to South Yarra for an audition for a television commercial.
Afterwards, I felt compelled to once again visit those places.
Again, there were tears.
Only this time, the tears were for a pain so deep and unbearable that it feels as if I shall weep for all time.
Now when I look for you, I will never be able to find you.
Nor hear your voice.
Nor see your beautiful face.
Nor touch your beautiful hands.
Nor lie next to your slender frame, held in your gentle embrace by tender loving arms.
I remember the sound of your breath as you lay sleeping beside me, the rise and fall of your chest, the soft brown hair on your olive toned legs.
Legs whose feet barely knew the constriction of shoes during these last years.
I remember the funny little things, your toes, knees, your strong gentle hands, the way you would pull back your long brown hair off your face, your beautiful brown eyes.

Now when I visit those places and remember those things it is no longer from the comfort of knowing that although there are miles between us, the bond is there, strong, resilient, confirmed in the very sharing of our breath, of the knowledge that we each take in sustaining and life giving oxygen from the same air, each breathing in or out as the other breathes in and out; our hearts beating in time with each other; each knowing that the other is always there.

No.

You are no longer there.

I can never again set eyes upon your beauty nor hear your warm voice of sunshine.

You are no longer here.

You no longer share with me the air that we breathe. Your chest that gently rose and fell as you lay sleeping is now white dust and ashes. Your voice will never more resonate its warm vibrations in the expression of who you are in the here and now. Your beautiful brown eyes will never look upon the brilliance of a new day dawning, nor the setting of the sun as another precious day ends, and it becomes night.

Your eyes lost their light.

Your eyes ceased to see.

And now your eyes are forever gone.

We will never again set eyes upon each other,

For all that remains of you is white dust and ashes, and the fading image of a life that once was.

18th November 2002. Dream notes.

My mind keeps slipping and I hang on to reality as best I can
thinking that soon, perhaps soon, when I rest, I will heal......
Every night I dream about you.
And every night the dream is the same although the details may
be different.
I am looking for you.
I keep looking for you everywhere, frantically, fear and panic
rising in my chest like a tidal wave of drowning seawater.
I travel to places we have been, places we love, places that
were ours.
And I can feel your presence, with me, yet gone from these
places we cherished.
No matter how hard I look for you I cannot find you anywhere.
The pain is excruciating, unbearable.
The aching, the longing
Other times, I am with you. I am talking to you. Sometimes we
talk about your death. I speak about how hard I am doing it.
I know how much you hurt; how much you cried.
Knowing that I could have done more
And I know, that not doing more was why you died.
A howl of unbearable anguish pierces the quiet of the night
The sound of my own voice waking me from my nightmare
Into the living nightmare
That what I have dreamt is true.

Conversations

BEV

An intellectual appreciation of philosophies of life and death was not enough to prepare Bev for her sudden and tragic loss.

The experience of grief is like a yawning cave of emptiness. We might have been separated, but he was still there, so on issues that were important we could still communicate, we could still talk! You know, you've got kids, you share a lifetime of experience, you've got extended family, and while you may not be together 24/7, there's always that part of each other that you share.

I sort of had two phases to my grief. I lost him the first time when the relationship ended. I was the one who finished the relationship and it certainly wasn't because I fell out of love with him. I would always deeply love and respect him; I just wasn't prepared to live that life anymore. I felt that if anything he had betrayed himself, and I didn't like to see that, so there was enormous pain there for me. I had enormous grief, not just for the loss of the love of my life, but also for all those essences of family values. I went through a fairly difficult phase then.

And then, I lost him for the second time when he died.

We had read books like *Journey of Souls*, *Destiny of Souls*, and *Journey to the Light*, and to some extent you have an understanding of the philosophy about death, but not being able to hug somebody when you need a hug, for instance, or to be able to express the utter frustration when you come across things that have just been left in an absolute mess, is a whole other thing.

This kind of grief is utter emptiness; it's a pain, a physical pain, and it doesn't just hurt your heart, you are actually in physical pain.

I've had quite a deal of experience of death and grieving. I nursed my father through the last years of his life, and I nursed Peter's mother and father through the last years of their lives. And I also helped Peter's aunt, who lived next door and who had no children.

Yet no matter how much you're prepared for it, no matter how long you've got to build up for it, it doesn't actually stop the pain when it happens, because suddenly, there is no going back.

I don't believe there is anything that prepares you for that sense of loss when it actually happens. But the difference between Peter's death and the death of the other family members was that there was the opportunity to say goodbye, you knew the end is coming, and this extraordinary opportunity is a gift you are given. You can talk about everything you wanted to talk about and do most of everything you wanted to do. You have a time when you are given this gift of sharing your soul with somebody whose life is coming to an end. And they share with you, and it's the most amazing experience you can ever have. You still have the pain when they go but you know that you have done and said everything that is possible to say in that time.

But when you lose a partner or anybody and it's instantaneous, even though in your head you know that you've got to say everything when it needs to be said, do everything when it needs to be done, you still don't really. Even though you understand the philosophy on an intellectual level, you don't really live it fully, and in this case, because Peter and I had not seen very much of each other before his death, there were things that went unsaid. I had called him when his grandson was born, and he came into the delivery room afterwards. We shared a very special time there, and that was beautiful. But I found it very hard to see this incredible depth of sadness in his eyes at that time, of knowing what he had lost. It didn't matter whether he was happy in his new life, because there was an incredible pain there that was palpable. He was very good at hiding it from other people but he couldn't hide it from us. I could see into his soul.

As he said to me, he had made enormous mistakes and he didn't know how to fix them, and it's hard to lose somebody when you know that that's how they're feeling at the end of their life, rather than having somebody who you've nursed through those last times knowing they've done all they can do. This is different. Here was an amazing person with an enormous capacity to understand life's journey in an incredible way, yet feeling great sadness at a time when he should have been enjoying life. We'd made such plans, things we were going to do and then suddenly we weren't doing them. In that sense, everyone's grief is different, but for me it was seeing him not happy. I would have dearly loved to see him blissfully happy, but that's not what I saw, so that's my thing that I have to deal with.

Just because you're not with the person it doesn't mean

that you stop caring and particularly not when he is the father of your children. And there is the enormous sadness too, in the fact that he won't be there to see his grandchildren grow up. You can't spend twenty-eight years of your life with someone and not be deeply affected when they're not around anymore.

KERRI

The once private life that Jeff and Kerri enjoyed was now subject to the scrutiny of the outside world.

I can remember thinking days after Jeff died, "I am moving one day closer to being happy again." I suppose it was to do with having something to look forward to, instead of wallowing in my predicament.

I lost all my privacy, which was hard when we were a fairly private couple. Privacy in my home, my finances, bringing up my children, my feelings, I was an open book. Some people would ask straight out about how much money I had, or if I owned my home now; or they'd tell me how lucky I was that I owned my home! A lot of people felt they were helping me by disciplining my children even when I was right there with them. I have no problem if I'm not in the room or not there at all, but it's almost as though because Jeff isn't there, they'll step in like I'm not even there, which is weird.

I had so many visitors after Jeff died which was very touching and for which I am eternally grateful. Some days I wasn't even dressed when they arrived! Often I couldn't get dinner organised, or I would just lose time with the daily routines, and friends would help out with these things. Luckily I'm not a routine or organised person, or this would have been quite a challenge.

I also found that I was (and still am) making myself do everything and go everywhere that people ask me; to dinners, to go visiting, to go here or there, whether I wanted to or not. I thought I should go because I felt that they wouldn't ask me anymore if I should turn them down. I remember one time in particular, when Claire was six weeks old, going to dinner in Fitzroy at night, to a restaurant that Jeff and I used to go to. I drove out at night in the pouring rain to this restaurant with my new baby! I remember sitting squashed in the corner and trying to breastfeed. There were people there whom I hadn't seen since Jeff died and they didn't mention him at all! I know it is hard to talk about, but it was an obvious thing to at least mention what had happened and I think it made it even more embarrassing and awkward that the truth got completely ignored, as though he had never died! Another time, I remember going to a BBQ and it started flaming and someone yelled, "Quick! We need a fireman!" That felt awful. It wasn't very sensitive. And it makes me especially sad when I go out with other families and the kids are running up to their dads crying, "Daddy, Daddy!" My kids don't have their daddy anymore.

Looking back, I don't know how smart it was to go out to these things, given the circumstances and how I was feeling at the time.

What made these nights going out even more difficult was that I hated staying home on my own, and I especially hated coming home to a dark and empty house. It reinforced my feelings of being alone, of being by myself and the fact that Jeff was no longer there. This sounds strange given that I was married to a fireman who was away nights on shift work, but after three and a half years, I think I am only just beginning to get used to it now. Occasionally, I still lay awake listening to every noise. Perhaps it was lucky I was sleep deprived with a new baby in the beginning, so that when I went to bed I generally fell asleep quickly.

LINDA

Adjusting to life without Rick was a process filled with anguish and pain.

I miss Rick in many ways, you know. One of our main duelling points in life was the swimming pool in our garden and of course I took no responsibility and no care and used it a lot; that was always Rick's domain. He used to whinge about it shockingly and I just thought, "Oh, you are being such a pain!" But now I understand why he did, to the point where if I ever sell this home it will be because of this wretched swimming pool.

I miss his intellect most of all. And I miss him at night, of course, being in bed on my own. I really miss him a lot then. I miss the comfort of his presence.

He had his own business and it operated from a really lovely flat or a little office that we put in our garden and he

107

spent a lot of time there, particularly in the evenings when he'd get home from somewhere. And it was just a wonderful comfort if I was in the house, knowing that he was out there, that his presence was always there and it's this presence that's gone, that sense of him just being there. Even now I sometimes think to myself, "Oh, Rick's just out in the office!" even though it's been well over twelve months. And it has been very hard to come to terms with this, because he was in hospital for that six months prior, and then he would come home every weekend or every second weekend and so I was used to him not being there and some days I still catch myself thinking he is there.

The other thing is that his illness and then his death were both so public; it was in all the papers. There were thousands and thousands of emails and letters and cards, literally, when he got ill. This was grief in itself, and then having to go though all that again with his death was very difficult.

I miss his smell, his warmth at night in the bed, all those kind of things; I miss his incredible, analytical, wonderful intellect.

Sometimes I think Rick's channelling through me, and I find myself thinking, "Oh, I sound just like Rick!" or dealing with situations exactly the way in which he would have.

One of the things I learnt with Rick's illness and his subsequent death was how to be patient.

ROSE

It was crucial that Rose find ways of releasing her distress so that she could be fully available for her now fatherless children.

The first six months were numb.

I used to take the kids to school, and I would come home, and I would cry and cry and cry. And cry. I would let it out, because I knew I had my time and place to do it in. I needed to be alone. And once I had done that, I could be focussed and there for the kids, and then I'd pick them up from school.

I believe that when there are feelings that are not healthy, then it's good to let them out, not to bottle them up. It's like filtering the scum off soup, you know, when you are making soup, you can either leave it there or remove it, but if you leave it there, the soup is not quite the same. And if it builds up it's not a good idea either. So you remove it, and then it's clear again. You need to remove the negative build-up or it can become dangerous. You're clearing yourself to be able to deal with all of the other things more competently. And I felt the children relied on me, they really needed their mum.

With his death, I acknowledged that I had contributed to his pain but I wasn't going to accept responsibility for his actions. This was not an easy thing to do. There were a lot of difficult times, particularly in terms of how other people responded to his death. As I said, suicide is very confusing, and there are so many unanswered questions. You have to live with these questions. Every day. And there never really are any answers.

But the hardest thing for me has been talking about it

with the kids. How do you explain something like suicide to a child? I try to teach them to be independent, to have emotional intelligence, to be able to deal with things in a positive way. There is no father figure for them, and they see other dads and families, so it's important for me to focus on experiences with their dad that had been wonderful, and also with my own father, to somehow create something positive in place of the sadness. It's hard for the kids, not having a dad, or a male figure in their lives.

JUNE

Losing her confidence in simple daily activities underpinned June's sense of unreality as she grappled with David's passing.

My immediate reaction to David passing away was that I got shitty with everybody. I thought they should be feeling the way I was feeling. And life should be for them as it was for me, whereas it wasn't like that. Everybody was living their life as if nothing had happened! As David said, life goes on, but this didn't make sense to me. And so I got shitty because, I'm thinking to myself, "Why aren't these people feeling the way I'm feeling? Why aren't they doing what I'm doing? I'm sitting here feeling miserable, crying my eyes out, so why aren't they doing that? They should be doing that because I've just lost my husband; we've all just lost someone close to us, so why aren't people crying like I am? Life should not be going on like normal!" I didn't understand how it could.

But I felt like that about so many things. For instance, if I went to the shopping centre, I would be thinking, "Why aren't people feeling like me? If I am so sad, how can you be happy? Why are you even shopping?" These are perfect strangers, mind you, and yet there I was, thinking that they had no right to be happy if I was feeling so miserable. I was like that for quite a while.

It was very isolating, to start off with, with things like my friends, for example. We have a circle of friends and all of our kids grew up together. We still see them, our kids still see them, and they're all still partners. And out of our little clique, I was the only one who didn't have a partner anymore. I was the only one who had been through anything of this sort. So I never went out. And I felt strange. If I went to a function where they were all there with their partners, it would just hit me, the pain and the sadness. It made me feel so alone. I went to one of the kid's weddings, and I was sitting at a table where they were all couples and I was the only female with no partner. It was very uncomfortable. And yet I'd known these people for years and years. They probably didn't notice anything. As far as they were concerned it was just me there. But I didn't feel comfortable.

I lost all my confidence in everything. Completely. I had no confidence at all. Even doing simple things around the house, or something like picking out a colour of paint for a wall! You know, once upon a time I'd have said that such and such was going to be green, that something else was going to be purple, yellow, or whatever. It was simple. And if I wanted alterations, I knew exactly what to do. I'd only have to say to David, "Can you do such and such?" and he would say, "That's going to be difficult." But he'd go away and think about it, and later say, "Oh yeah, I could do that." Whereas after he'd gone, I'd be thinking, "Oh, I don't know if I should do that purple, or change this or that." I had trouble with making simple decisions.

And I had that issue of confidence with everything, even with things that I said. I was just completely shattered, completely shattered. Even driving, even just getting into the car and driving somewhere, I had no self-confidence.

In fact, especially with something like driving! David would never ever get lost. He had a good sense of direction, whereas I didn't. If he did get lost he would be able to find his way back again, whereas I always got lost. But I didn't panic. It didn't worry me. I'd just stop the car and get out and ask somebody. Whenever we were driving about together, I just used to sit in the car and do the sight-seeing bit, you know, "Oh, did you see that!" and he'd say, "No, I'm driving!" And so I never took any notice of where I was going or how to get to somewhere.

Not now.

I don't know why it happens, and I've heard other women say the same thing, that they completely lose their confidence. Not necessarily if their husband or partner has died but even in a separation, or a divorce, they completely lose their self-confidence. It's been seven years, and I'm only now just beginning to have some confidence in myself again, to be able to do things by myself.

But I miss him, and it's in so many, many ways. I miss cooking a meal for him; cooking tea for two is now tea for one.

Or baking for him: he was a real 'sweet' person, he loved his sweets and he loved his cake. And now I don't bake anymore. I might do if the kids are coming over, but other than that, I just don't bake. Nor can we go for a walk together with the dog. And I miss going over to see our son or daughter together, catching up with them, or visiting friends. We used to go ballroom dancing and I don't go dancing anymore. I really miss that because it used to be a social evening too. It's a partnership, it's doing things in twos, it's everything: his cutting the grass and me raking it; my making a cup of tea, and both of us sitting outside together on the bench seat in the afternoon with a cup of tea and some biscuits. And sometimes he'd sit there and fall asleep, but it didn't matter, because he was there. It's me going crook at him for singing all the time. I'd tell him, "Oh for God's sake, would you stop singing that song!" because he'd be practising his barbershop music, and as soon as he got up, he'd be singing. And I used to tell him to shut up. And now, it wouldn't matter, he could sing as much as he liked. That would be the least of my worries. I miss the sound of him singing in the house.

Just having him around, just having him here. It's everything. It's life! He was my life!

My life will never be the same; never. It can't be. How can it be the same? As time goes on, you just learn to cope with it better. I can still put on a smile and do crazy things and all that, but my life will never be the same and there will always be the sadness, this empty part of my life where David used to be.

ELWYN

Elwyn's world was turned upside down with Cathy gone.

When Cathy died I felt as if I had a hole in my chest the size of a basketball. My life felt so empty: Cathy was my love, my life, and my everything, and now she had been taken away.

Every morning I would wake up and for a moment expect her to be lying in bed next to me or in the other room. I would then have to face the reality that she wasn't there, and focus instead on my three kids.

My eldest daughter Katie was seventeen and had her year twelve exams approaching. She would put the washing on in the morning as soon as she woke up. Before she went to school she would hang it out, and in the evening bring in the clothes, and iron them. My younger daughter Jacinta, unlike Katie, refused to have any counselling. She went off the rails a bit and I was constantly getting calls from the school to inform me of the trouble she had been in. Although they knew about her circumstances, she was often in detention and getting suspended. I wished Cathy were around as I felt I was already failing as a father. Jacinta soon quit school and got a full time job at the age of fifteen. My son Ryan was thirteen, and didn't say much. He refused to have any counselling as well, but I knew he was missing his mum.

I felt lost without Cathy around. We had Christmas presents in our wardrobe wrapped up, and I had no idea what was in them or who they were intended for. I had no clue how and where she got the kids' schoolbooks for their next year. I was concerned the kids were not eating correctly. I had trouble making simple decisions on my own, like what colour do I paint the bathroom? Or what brand of microwave oven should I buy? I didn't have anyone to sit and talk to about my day at work. I had to try and remember to buy presents for relatives' birthdays … the list goes on and on.

I had a lot advice from relatives and friends on how to bring up my kids. I would get asked how I was, and when I replied that I was okay, they would ask me how I was really going. At the annual Firemen's Ball I attended, I would get a few of the wives would come up and talk to me and ask me if I wanted to dance. I felt like I had a sign on me saying, "This poor man is a widower, please feel sorry for him and ask him for a dance!"

Thankfully that is not as common now.

PAUL S

Paul cherishes the bittersweet memories of his and Delina's life together.

The best words to describe my life without Delina are: Emptiness, because she is no longer here; Loneliness, because I have no children; and Guilt, because I am still alive and feel in some ways that I let Delina down. She kept a diary for the last fourteen years of her life. Maybe I should have taken a sneak look at her diary, especially in 2006. She knew she was seriously ill but did not use the word cancer. I should have realised that it was more than just anorexia.

My life changed from being a truly happily married man to a broken, sad and lonely widower.

I have huge regrets that we didn't talk more openly about Delina's illness and that she was dying. I guess we did not want to upset each other. I never knew what her wishes were for after her passing. I did say to her that I would like for there to be a Catholic funeral and for her to be dressed in her wedding dress and that her ashes would be scattered in the Sydney harbour and that I would eventually end up there myself. And yet she never told me what she wanted.

I am extremely hurt that some of my family members didn't bother coming to Delina's funeral or even to send bereavement cards. Delina always remembered birthdays and Christmas time, yet this was rarely reciprocated, and didn't get much better after she died. This has caused me great sadness.

Recently, I went to Sydney and visited the place where I scattered Delina's ashes. I threw a single rose into the water from the ferry. I visited some of her friends, and I also went to revisit some of the places we used to go to. This brought back sweet but such sad memories.

While I was in Sydney, I stayed in the Greystanes Inn where I stayed when I first went to meet Delina all those years ago. It brought back a flood of sad, sweet memories that made me weep.

I wear Delina's rings on a chain around my neck and still proudly wear my wedding rings. I have some degree of hearing loss. In many ways, Delina was my hearing. I miss not putting my left hand in Delina's right hand as we walked.

It is particularly hard to come home to an empty house. There is no one there to greet me and talk about my day with. I don't like eating alone, or sleeping alone.

I miss her beautiful smile, our intimacy, just being with her.

I don't like knowing that I can never see and touch her and be with her again.

ERIKA

The loss of normal emotional coping mechanisms was one of many difficulties Erika faced after Damian's death.

I don't remember much after Damian died, not of those next few months. There are glimpses of memory; there was darkness all around. I kept doing stuff but I don't know how. I must have been in a trance. I kept conducting choir; I even played with our band; I had lots of visitors and I didn't mind that.

I took sleeping pills at night that the nurse at the hospital had given me. That was good. I read everything I could find about people whose partner had died. It helped me to make it real. I felt like a complete oddity. I no longer fitted anywhere; I felt like I stuck out like a sore thumb. I had the feeling everyone looked at me differently. I looked at myself differently. One day, at the local supermarket, a young woman approached me and introduced herself. Her husband had died of a brain tumour. We stood by the bread stand and cried together.

I needed to tell people what had happened, in order to

believe it myself. I called people in Palestine, England, the United States, and Germany. When I rang Abu Hassan in Jerusalem, all he could say, about two dozen times, was "Shit – shit, shit, shit – shit!" No one could have said it better.

I needed and wanted to know how other people had found out about Damian's death; others in the family, friends. I needed to hear that a friend on the other side of the globe had wept inconsolably for the loss of Damian and for me. The image of their grief has become part of my image of my friends, and it makes me feel closer to them. I still want to know how people found out, to understand that their life was also changed forever at that moment, just like mine.

When Damian died, the shock was absolute. It took away many of my normal coping mechanisms. I couldn't make decisions, I didn't deal with stress well, and there was no prospect of happiness in sight. Someone told me not to make any important decisions in the first year, and that was good advice. I don't know how I survived that year. I was carried by family and friends.

By the end of that first year I had what I needed to get me through the next: a group of friends, themselves younger widows, with whom I could talk about the loss of my previous life. And the boys had found other kids who had lost a Dad. That experience of not being alone in this situation and being able to continue to talk about our loss when others gradually stopped asking, was the most important achievement of the first year. We called our group 'WithoutYou' – a name I still find difficult to say out loud. I sometimes think it should be called WithYou, because it helps us to live on WithYou, WithoutYou.

ANN

The darkness of the winter in which Patrick's life had ended contrasted with the arrival of new life in springtime.

Time felt arrhythmic after Patrick died. The days seemed to be rapid, and yet long. I felt continually pulled back and forth between the freshness and rawness of the emotions I felt when he died, and the casual humour of normality.

After Patrick died, I stayed at my brother Ian's for about four weeks and I just didn't want to go home at all. We used to live in this tiny, tiny flat, and I just did not want to go back there. My parents looked after our dogs for that time.

I stayed away from work as well during that period. I think I just used my sick leave, and then I went back to work. It was about a month after he died, because I went back to work around the same time that I went home to our flat. And I was due for night shift but I only lasted six out of seven nights because they were long night shifts, twelve-hour night shifts. I started at a quarter to eight at night, and finished about a quarter past eight in the morning and then drove home exhausted, over the Westgate Bridge through all the traffic. I could never sleep during the day because there was always someone out there with a whipper snipper or a chainsaw, or some little boy next door making pretend fire engine noises or some other noisy interruption.

After that I just went on sick leave and I hung out in the flat or in the garden because it was spring and I planted things. And the tulips Patrick had planted all came up.

I took some photos of his tulips. He'd planted other things as well. He liked those little miniature violas and pansies, those small, delicate flowers. It was funny, for a big man, he liked all these prissy little flowers, whereas I liked flowers with a little more substance. He always used to crack me up. He was such a big, blokey bloke, and then he had this old-fashioned grandma and girly taste in flowers!

Patrick died at the end of winter, and in springtime, his tulips came up. And that was nice.

So I sat out there under the big ash tree and read and watched videos and sewed and made quilts.

The service took me three weeks to organise. We had it down at the Queenscliff Fort. There is an embankment overlooking the water and we had the service there under the flagpole, which was really lovely. And the band that was at our wedding played there in the hall. I said to them, "You were at my wedding. Do you think you could play at my husband's funeral?" I don't suppose they often get asked to play at too many funerals. It was the 'Band Who Knew Too Much!' The only person who sort of bopped along was my two-year-old nephew. Everyone else looked either shocked or bewildered.

But that was it. I just couldn't do a funeral. You're meant to just have a funeral and pack them all off in a week? I couldn't have done that. I never saw him after I saw him in the hospital. They shoved him off to the mortuary, and I never saw him again. He was there for three weeks. It was as though I had just detached from his body. I just couldn't have a body there; after all, he was gone. I couldn't be physically reminded.

It was six months before I was able to bring his ashes home.

I remember them seeming really heavy, but it was a bizarre thing to think that this was him. Even now it seems peculiar, to contemplate that that was the entirety of this person. I found that if I actually tuned into what it was, it was quite bizarre: was this the mortal remains of what was once a person?

And I suppose now when I think about it, it helps me get that disconnect between the body and everything else. The body is not really relevant. And yet there's so much we attach to the body isn't there? When he died, and the nurses do what they do, put the flower on his chest, and whatever else it is that they do, and I walk in and they try to tell me how peaceful he looks, but to me, it wasn't him. That body was not him! So I don't know why it took me six months to be able to bring his ashes home.

Since Patrick died, people have often asked me how I am or how I'm coping and I feel a bit like I've had a big part of me chopped off or perhaps, more aptly, paralysed as if I've had a stroke. There's a whole part of me that's on hold, that has atrophied, and I have to rehabilitate myself to be able to work wholly again.

Every day has been about taking lots of single steps, rarely on the same path, yet always on the same journey.

PAUL B

In unfamiliar territory, Paul was haunted by reminders of the life he had shared with Leanne.

Leanne's death propelled me into a nightmare I was ill-equipped to deal with, although I doubt anyone can ever be 'equipped' for such things. I had the lives of four young kids to deal with and now I was a widower. I have many wonderful people who supported me and indeed who kept me going in an otherwise hopelessly bleak landscape. My weight plummeted to an all time low, and the swift onset of major depression was devastating. I was ready to follow Leanne.

I remember not being able to go into our bedroom any more as I was so overwhelmed by everything. All her things were all around me but not her. I removed a large family photo board from the wall: I couldn't face the reminder that the world that once was, the world that was my life, my reality, our reality, was now gone. I would rise every day and make a cup of tea, and then I wrote in my journal, and then I would read. I managed to get through each day by expending no more energy than was needed, and each hour was broken into fifteen minute segments. If this was unmanageable, then I would endure by living life three to five minutes at a time.

And it did get worse. I finally reached a stage where one time my little one needed Daddy so much but I could no longer bear to hear her cries. I couldn't get out of bed. My brother arrived one morning to check in and found me unable to move on my own. Shortly after, I started anti-depressant medication.

After Leanne's passing I was without an identity or a map of this new, alien landscape in which I found myself. I was petrified. I felt that no one knew me – and they didn't, at least on the inside. I was now a stranger to everything and everyone, including myself. If I was not Leanne's partner, then who the hell was I? I was an empty tin can. No one was home. Small things became mountainous, like how to cook, what to cook with my energy so low; how could I deal with the kids schooling? My resources to cope were stretched to their limit.

I was gripped with an unbelievable sadness, realising little things, like I would never again see Leanne's clothing go though the wash, or hear her sweet welcome when I arrived home, or hear her call the kids for dinner. I remember the yearning to hold her becoming so intolerable that I was powerless to manage it, and in the night the yearning became my worst enemy. I craved for her physically and emotionally. It was overwhelming. I never imagined I'd be put to the limits of my endurance in this way. I remember thinking to myself, "So, now I am a dead man walking!" because that was how it felt. I was the living embodiment of the saying, "Even though a man should die, yet shall he live."

5

A Strange New World: change

When we move beyond the immediacy of death, a new period of mourning begins. A different experience of grief is encountered now.

Perhaps we become more aware of the world beyond our direct surroundings, whereas up until this time our focus and energy has been solely on the challenge of placing one foot in front of the other, of simply getting through each day.

While we may still struggle to get though our days, we now find space enough to catch our breath. And yet, once we begin to breathe again, we notice that things have changed.

Or, at least, we have.

In this place, our relationship with the outside world slowly begins to shift, and our experience of loss is integrated into a new sense of reality.

Journal Entry

December 30th, 2002.
Recognising slowly
Incrementally
That what was part of a continuum
Is now part of the past
History
A rough cloth bag
Full of remnants and bric-a-brac held together
By an invisible glue
Of memory

I feel so alone.

Friends, or people who I thought were friends, are no longer
there because their presence in my life, it seems, was based on
a shallow connection. People's response to and regard for me
continually surprises me. Angers me!
I spoke with Sam last night and told him how miserable I was
feeling and to my utter disbelief he responded, "Still?" as though
I could have somehow packed up my sorrow in a suitcase and
put it away like warm winter clothes.
He behaved the same way when Jimmy died. He obviously has
not experienced the depth of anguish one feels with such a loss.
Or if he has, then he evidently has no compassion for others
because he certainly doesn't show it.
Then there was Roberto! At a shoot I was working at with him on
Sunday, there was a band playing, and they played a beautiful,

moving song and it brought tears to my eyes. It was a little
awkward having an emotional reaction like this in public, but
the emotional tone of the song triggered a flashback of such
intensity, a vivid and almost palpable recollection of you singing
into a microphone, your warm and husky voice, of music, of gigs
and performing and of the world we once inhabited, that I was
momentarily overcome with such sadness. When I innocently
shared this with my so-called friend, hoping perhaps for a little
compassion for my still-raw feelings, he contemptuously snapped,
"But look at how wonderful the day is. The sun is shining, it
is a beautiful day! How can you possibly be sad on such a
beautiful day?"
What an idiot! Yes, the sun is shining but my Stu is not here, alive
in this beautiful day!
The sun is shining, but my heart bleeds! Oh how my
heart bleeds!

After such encounters, there has emerged for me, something of
a measure by which to assess the quality of a connection with a
person. If someone is empty, draining, and lacking in compassion
and empathy, then I have little time for them.
I have come to appreciate, in a whole new way, those
connections with people that have a sense of truth
about them.
It seems I have such little patience these days. I see things
differently now.
Very differently.
But lately, I have also been having bad thoughts and I find myself
caring less and less about things. Like I find myself hoping that

something really bad happens to all the idiots who have said stupid things like, "The sun is shining; it is a beautiful day!" or "You'll get over it," or "I know how you feel, my grandfather passed away last year," or, "Well that's closure for you, isn't it!" rather than, "I'm so sorry about your loss. Are you okay?" Are these people for real? I never used to be the kind of person to wish bad things on people. This is not right.

The best comment by far has to be from the vicar's wife, when I dropped-in to the church one day in search of a moment's solace at the place where we were married. On the way in, the woman approached me, cornering me in the car park, so I politely enquired as to whether she had heard news of your death, in the hope she might get the hint that I wanted to be alone.

Answering in the affirmative, she looked me in the eyes and said, in all earnestness, "It must be such a blessed relief!"

I was dumbstruck! It took some time to scrape my jaw off the ground and dignify the comment with a response. Since when has dying become any kind of solution to one's struggles? Oh yes, thank you! We're all so much better off now that Stu has buggered off and we can get on with our lives! Pardon me, but aren't you people supposed to offer comfort in these situations? I don't care how well meaning the remark may have been, this was callous and unthinking. Who are these absolute, utter idiots?

I feel more and more like I just don't care anymore! I don't particularly like this world at all. I just don't see the point of it all. I really don't. I know I sound very grumpy but I feel like my heart is completely smashed and that my arms and legs are filled with lead, weighing me down into the ground.

Conversations

BEV

The public perception of Peter Brock created additional stress for Bev to cope with after his death.

We've had to deal with quite a few things since Peter's death. For instance there have been claims of illegitimate children, and I sit here and wonder sometimes. One of the things that surprised me was that because Peter had a public profile, there were lots of people wanting to claim ownership of part of him after his death. It's like his presence in their life, no matter how fleeting, took on greater importance than it actually had had. I don't have any problem with that; I think it's fantastic that they saw him as an amazing person whom they wanted to be part of their life. But the perspective for some of them was all wrong; they had an incredible and inappropriate sense of ownership over him.

Most of the time I could just ignore what was going on, but there were times when I couldn't, because it was as if his death was being used for personal gain. So, people emerged wanting to write books about him and claiming lifelong friendship with him and I know that these weren't lifelong friends because I had known Peter's life intimately. And there were a couple of people involved who certainly were not life long friends, and so I endlessly had to deal with people wanting to cash-in on an association with Peter – however inconsequential. The 'marketing' skills of people of this sort just staggered me at times. They were literally 'cashing-in' – flogging stuff even. Suddenly there were speedboats and jet skis that were all part of the so-called Brock Production Line which had never existed, but somehow (fake) signatures would appear and these things were apparently Peter's. And I'd sit there, completely astonished that all this could be going on. People who aren't in the public eye would not have to deal with a lot of this sort of madness.

There are some very enterprising people in this world. I found women out there who had been in love with him or whatever, and they felt the need to come and tell me, almost to ask me for forgiveness. And so at a time when my emotions were raw, I had an onslaught of all these confessions. At times it was very bizarre, and in some ways, to be honest, I really felt sad for a lot of these people. They had to create something artificial in order to feel good. So I guess there really are a lot of bizarre things that go on. And yet, people who are grieving in ordinary circumstances in life, when they haven't had a public profile, can have bizarre things happen to them, too.

Death does amazing things to people, and I never realised quite the impact it could have on people's attitude to money, for example, to possessions, and on their sense of ownership of a person. People say things and handle things in their own way but some of it can actually be quite cruel. And that amazes me. I think that they're grieving themselves so that they don't think of the impact that some of the things they're saying can have on others. These people are in the minority, I have to say, because most people are just amazing; most people are incredible. But there are always going to be some people who overstep boundaries. There are times when the human race absolutely staggers me.

But then I stop and remind myself how fortunate I am to be in this position. There are some terrible things happening in this world; it can be a pretty sad place. By comparison, I've got nothing to complain about, I'm in heaven. And so, the best thing for me to do is just walk away from people who are negative. I feel for them. I empathise with them. I don't always agree with how they're doing things, but I really don't like seeing people trying to make gains out of Peter's name and reputation. But then, they always did it when he was alive so I guess I should to be used to that. At least it won't go on forever. I remind myself that some day it'll disappear, because eventually it all goes away. And then they have to find somebody else to try to make a living out of.

KERRI

Being busy as a sole parent caring for her children does little to combat Kerri's sense of being alone.

I think the loneliness is really hard. There is no one that I can talk to intimately, so I end up talking about things to people I would never have before, because I need to get things out. And then I find myself going over and over incidents and trying to work out if I've said something or done something to upset people, whereas if Jeff were there he would just say, "Don't worry, forget about it." This is my own lack of confidence too, but when you're in a relationship, it is so good to be able to come home and just talk: losing that takes a while to get used to.

It is also difficult having the sole responsibility for your children, making decisions on schooling, discipline, caring, listening, transporting, feeding, clothing, birthdays, Christmases. This year I'm finding it really hard as Sarah is off to secondary school, so it is all new: uniforms, school books, orientation days and also her graduation from primary school. I try really hard to take everything in so I can enjoy the moments and remember them, but I feel I am just flying by the seat of my pants and not really able to take it all in. Liam will continue primary school and Claire starts three-year-old kinder one morning a week. I will have two and a half hours free each week, childless. I will have three different pick-ups and deliveries, so it is going to be a busy couple of years ahead.

I often say to the kids, "Lucky I don't have a life!" because I am completely consumed with their activities!

LINDA

A strong network of support provides the backdrop for the way in which Linda chooses to deal with her bereavement.

I've been very deliberate about dealing with grief, and I've done that through very regular grief counselling. I've had real guidance. I've used anti-depressants for six or eight months and done so under a really fabulous family doctor whom I've been seeing about once a month. I've made a very deliberate effort to do this is over these past twelve months. For the first time in twenty years I've done regular exercise and I've learnt meditation; I have enjoyed a good gin and tonic every now and again, but I don't beat myself up about stuff like that, I just don't. I take care of my body; I look after myself. And I have an incredible, demanding role and that is certainly a great diversion.

I have relied on people. I've not pretended; I'm not a big screamer or crier, I haven't done much of that. I don't know if this happens to others, but my grief counsellor said it would happen, and it did: one day the dams just burst. I was on holidays and it was the day before we did his ashes and everything was all perfect. I was in a small little town and in the holiday house by myself at the time, and I just screamed and yelled and got angry at him and cried for about twenty or thirty minutes resulting in my throwing up. It was the most amazing purge, and it was incredible because the next day we did his ashes.

ROSE

For Rose, the difficulty of raising her children without their father has been one of many challenges.

Some people don't come here anymore, because they can't deal with it, or with seeing us. It took a long time before they did come to visit. In the earlier years, (and it was mainly men), people just looked at us, the girls and me together, and it's as though they were wondering why Andrew went and did what he did, leaving us like that. You can see that they get angry that we're in this situation, that we have been left as we are.

It's the children who see other dads and their families, and at times this can be difficult. So I've always had discussions with them about their dad, and they've shared their thoughts and feelings and experiences. If there have to be daily conversations, then we have them and we talk about it. There's a great sadness there for them, especially in the beginning. I feel for them.

Sometimes I see couples there that don't even do half the job that I do on my own. There's constant arguing about how they should do things for the kids, there's a constant battle, and the one thing I can't stand hearing is married mums complain that they do everything on their own! It's as though their husbands are not even around. They don't appreciate that simply the presence alone of somebody, in and of its self, is so much more than they realise. They really seem to take things so much for granted.

And then there are those that say we're better off that he died, because their own life has been living hell with their ex-husbands after a divorce. I look at them and I think, "You have no idea! You have absolutely no idea!"

JUNE

Fear of being 'the odd one out' and having loneliness as a constant companion are a couple of the uninvited guests in June's new life.

I don't go out on my own. Because for me to be a single woman, at my age anyway, I feel uncomfortable, although nowadays it is more acceptable for a woman to go out on her own. I mean, you can go out, and have a drink in a bar on your own, whereas years ago you couldn't do that.

I still go shopping at one of those big shopping centres and I watch couples, especially ones around my age. And I watch them and I envy them because they don't realise how lucky they are! And I think, "That should be us! That should be David and me doing that! We should be doing that still." Sometimes I will go in to the centre, but then I have to come out again because it is too upsetting. I just can't stay there.

I envy those people, not in a nasty way; I envy them that bliss of ignorance.

And I still feel like that, you know, and I felt that only yesterday. I was taking my grandchildren back home from a sleepover. It was such a beautiful day, and I was coming home through Jumping Creek Road and it's such a pretty drive and I just burst into tears. I kept thinking, "This should be David

135

and me driving home!" I just felt that he should have been there driving home with me from our daughter's house, dropping the grandchildren off with me. I suppose too because everybody's out on a Sunday: it's a lovely day, the convertible cars have their roofs down, and they're all partners. They're all partners, and I'm driving home on my own! This is so unfair. Why? Why did it have to happen?

With this whole experience, it's like there's a tap, and somebody has turned it off. And suddenly you don't know what to do. I was lost. It made me panicky. As I said, with everyday things, you lose the confidence in doing them, and yet you've been doing these things for years, things that had been second nature! I was no longer involved with the theatre company because of my lack of confidence. It took two years before I felt confident enough to become involved again. What also made this enormously difficult was my knowing all the people at the theatre company. And I couldn't cope emotionally with seeing them and being around them when David wasn't there. They were a very big part of David's and my life; if we weren't doing *Follies*, then we were doing tickets for them.

So it was at least two years before I had enough confidence to get back up on stage. At first I only did front of house. That was the initial opening for me to get involved. I think I may have done a couple of nights to begin with, and then the following year I got up on stage.

Perhaps I need to move out, make a new break, join a new theatre company and start a new life. Maybe that's the next chapter, I don't know. But I don't have the confidence yet to do that.

It's a security thing in many ways. I'm secure here. I know everything here. This is my little haven. You know, when I'm home I don't have to be somebody I don't feel like being that day. In here I can be who I want to be or do what I want. If I want to sit and cry, I can do that in here. When you get outside, you have to put this face on. People want to see your smile. They don't want to see you looking sad. Maybe it reminds them. Maybe they think you shouldn't be sad anymore. But you don't always feel like smiling.

So here, in my home, I'm secure. I can be however I want to be.

ELWYN

The loss felt by Elwyn is compounded by his children leaving home.

Since Cathy got sick and since she has died, I have become aware of how precious life really is. I don't want anything to happen to me, at least until my three kids are completely independent and able to take care of themselves. I have stopped taking unnecessary risks on the road and I go to the doctor's surgery for regular tests and checkups. On one occasion I had a bad stomach pain and I called an ambulance to take me to the hospital in case it was my appendix.

I have become more tolerant of people and their behaviour. I sometimes look at a person walking down the street, and they look quite normal – without a care in the world – yet they may have experienced a similar tragedy or maybe even a worse one than mine. I no longer get angry with people on the roads, or at work – if someone does the wrong thing – or if someone ignores me when I walk past them. Heaven only knows what was on their mind at the time; I have had my mind elsewhere and done similar things.

I feel more alone now than I have ever felt. I'm not just missing Cathy, but a lot of the time I'm home alone. My three kids have all grown up and now have their own cars, and most evenings, they go off with their friends.

Recently, I got myself a passport and so now do a lot of overseas travelling. This is something that never used to interest Cathy or me before. All our plans for when I was to retire went out the window when Cathy passed away.

I experienced a lot of sadness, and I still do experience this sadness; the sadness I felt when I lost Cathy. The worst feeling in the world is watching someone you love slowly dying and not being able to do anything about it.

There was so much sadness for me in seeing my three children's faces as they watched their mum in so much pain, and finally as they saw her pass away in my arms. My kids were so close to her. Even when they were in school, she would help out in the classroom with reading. She did canteen duty and often went with them on school excursions. She would take them to school, and wait for them at the gate after school. She lived for her children.

I felt sadness seeing the sorrow in Cathy's face as her condition worsened every day; knowing that she would never get to see or hold her grandchildren, something she had always dreamed about. Even when Cathy smiled, I could see the sadness and pain in her eyes.

On our twentieth wedding anniversary, twenty-six days before she died, Cathy hugged me for about five minutes. She thanked me for being a good husband and not leaving her when she got cancer. She met quite a few women at Peter Mac (the Peter MacCallum Cancer Centre) whose husbands had left them because they couldn't deal with the cancer. Cathy also kept apologising for the trouble and inconvenience her cancer has caused. I told her to stop being silly, and then she told me to make sure I married someone nice when she died. I told her to change the subject and that she wasn't going to die.

There is sadness in seeing the grief on my mother-in-law's face; watching her only daughter going through all that pain. Cathy was prescribed morphine, however we never filled the prescription, as Cathy wanted to have the pain and be aware of her surroundings, rather than be doped up to the eyeballs and not know what was going on.

We always went to a restaurant on any of our birthdays, and it was coming up to what would have been Cathy's fortieth birthday. We decided to still go although Cathy was no longer with us. I knew that this would be a really difficult time for all of us, especially my mother in law, so I decided to shave my head completely. There was still the sadness in her eyes, but I made a point of sitting opposite her and so my new haircut was a topic of conversation for most of the evening.

I can't say the sadness now is any different to the sadness I felt before. Perhaps the difference for me is the regularity with which it occurs. It took about eighteen months before I actually felt that I had become a single person and Cathy was no longer living with me. I started to make decisions on my own and was getting used to a new 'normal' life.

We have a lot of family photos around the house and in my room, and every time I looked at Cathy it would make me feel sad. That doesn't happen as often now. The sadness is there still but mainly on special occasions or milestones in my kids' lives: when the kids got their licences, or when it was their first day at work, or Katie's twenty-first birthday and her engagement. I don't know as yet how I will cope walking her down the aisle on her wedding day and her mum not being there to see how beautiful she will look.

I was very happy before – I had a well-paying, enjoyable job, a big house to live in, many good friends, good health, and most of all a loving wife and mother of my three beautiful children. My happiness was complete and felt permanent.

Although I am generally a happy person, at the end of the day the person who played the biggest part in my happiness is no longer there. Now the happiness feels incomplete and short lived. Whenever I am enjoying myself on a holiday or any special occasion for example, I always long for Cathy to be there to admire the scenery or enjoy the music and dancing with me.

I would gladly give up all of my possessions, even my own life, if that would bring Cathy back.

PAUL S

Learning new life skills has been essential to Paul's adapting to life as a widower.

In some ways, I seem to have become quite bitter. Also angry. I sometimes become angry very easily and have little tolerance for people if they cross me. I react differently to things compared to how I used to. Maybe it's that I see the world in a different way.

I was quite suicidal in the early days. Less so now. I am getting some grief counselling and this helps, and I am also on anti-depressants, which helps as well.

I feel this real need to relate my life with Delina and her passing to other people. It's something that I want to talk about, but I don't think people want to hear me talk about it.

I have found that I have had to learn many things like running the finances, day-to-day shopping, and even silly things like the ironing. I always did the housework, but not the ironing, and I don't know which creases I am supposed to put in and which I am supposed to take out.

I have had to learn to deal with all the legal matters like notifying social security and changing over the title of the house, and for many of these things I would have had to produce Delina's death certificate. This has been painful.

Just driving past the hospital where she passed away is painful.

Sometimes, I still get mail for Delina. Sometimes I receive mail addressed to the executor of the late Delina Said. This makes me sad. It always brings home the finality of the life of my beautiful Delina.

Erika's world evolves into a new and unfamiliar form taking on some small changes and some large.

When Damian died of heart failure, suddenly and without any warning, my life as it had been ended. Looking back now, I can hardly recognise myself in the person I was before he died. Not only was I different, this town was also different, had flair to it, a romance about it. Streets, beaches, familiar houses seem different to me now – they actually look different even though they have not been altered. Some places change simply with the loss of familiarity, someone's home or a spot on the river where we used to spend time now seems different.

Our house has a different feel to it. The front window no longer bears the promise of seeing Damian's ute pull up after work. The place where he worked used to be filled with the expectation of seeing him in it – now it means nothing. Because I came to this town and country to be with him, most places were initially defined by an experience with him. Now, one by one, their feel is gradually overlaid with the experience of me being here by myself, and so they change.

I will not go to the first house we lived in when I first came to town. I want to keep the memory of it as a place where we were always together. I don't think I could bear not finding him there if I went.

I understand nothing about death. I don't know where the dying go, or what they get up to. But I know about Damian's love for me, strong and stubborn, ready to move the world, if that was what was needed. I know it because I knew him. But he was also accepting, of life, and death, and in his death, as I was holding him, I knew that he had accepted death. And that since he did, I should too. Can't say that I have, but one day I will.

I used to be scared of silly things, like being in the house by myself at night, or swimming across the river in murky water. The fear of deep water was gone after he died. Shockingly, it just disappeared. It seemed irrelevant to be afraid of the murky water when the worst that could possibly happen to me had already happened.

The night fear took longer, and had to be worked on; you can't live in fear all the time, can you? I used to lie in bed, listening to every creak and sound, petrified. Then I learned the trick with the radio; leaving it on in the background, even on static, to create a noise level to drown out the little creaks. That worked for a few months, until I realised I no longer needed it. Now I'm all right, I don't hear the worrying sounds anymore.

Some relationships have changed, though I sometimes find it surprising that many are actually still the same, when I have changed so much and feel so different about myself and the world. Reliance, even dependence on the people around me was very strong in the first years. I hadn't needed to build strong reliance's on others when Damian was still there because he was all I needed, although I had made a few good friends. But after his death, some relationships with friends and also his family became my anchor in life, steel ropes, holding me in place, indestructible, unwavering.

Others withered away, because they were carried by

Damian alone and the friendship didn't make the journey to me.

Others have changed, but have over time become my own, and are strong and reliable. The good experiences far outweigh the disappointing ones, although I have found that the second year was very much about dealing with relationships, re-defining them, building them, and sometimes letting them go.

There are some who carry his spirit; some who look out for me for him, with the same unwavering determination he had.

In them, he is alive.

ANN

A whirlwind of activity and new experiences consume Ann's attention; in some ways shifting focus away from her loss.

In 2001, I started my Doctorate of Psychology. I changed to casual status at work, so that I could do both. I had five days at week at uni, which was weird, but it was good. I was in amongst all these twenty-somethings, and crying, and they'd start talking about grief or something and I'd start crying, or I'd correct them all the time about things we were studying, like post traumatic stress disorder, and they'd have preconceptions about it and I would correct them all the time. It got to the stage where the lecturer would say something and everyone would look towards me, waiting to see what I would say. Being at university at that time in some ways was a good thing; it kind of saved me in a way. I couldn't stand being at work, and

I'd been planning to go to uni anyway.

I don't think my path was 'normal' if there is such a thing. Going to university was many years of hard, bloody slog. It was just a whole different experience, and at the end of it all, I came out of it with a whole different qualification and a whole different professional circle. There was nothing normal about those years and it was as though my whole life changed anyway. In some ways that may have prolonged the adjustment, but in some ways it might have actually facilitated it.

And it's really hard to tell because going to Uni was such a stressful thing to do anyway, but then our life was already really hard. It wasn't as if we were living together in a house that we owned, and had nice jobs, and then he died, and then things were ruined, and I had my community, and suddenly I was confronting this big change! On the contrary, we lived in a converted garage and both worked in poorly paying jobs for goodness' sake! There were lots of temporary sorts of things; there was nothing stable about our lives anyway, so any change after he died was possibly going to be for the better.

So there have been many changes. I had a lot of other stuff going on as well, finishing my doctorate, getting a job, moving into a place where there was plenty of room for the dogs, and finally being in a position where I could have people over.

Probably what was more significant in terms of change was our dog CJ dying about five months after moving out of the little flat. I was pleased to be leaving behind some of the poverty we had, of being in a position to move into a three bedroom house with my dogs, but then a few months later CJ got really sick and died, very expensively. CJ dying so suddenly was enormously upsetting, because he was such a strong connection with Patrick.

One day the mechanic had come around to collect Patrick's car to remove the bull bar and air horn. It was while I was still living in the flat, and CJ and Nellie were there, but I was out at the time. Apparently CJ was heard howling his heart out when he heard the car engine start. He just adored Patrick, absolutely adored him. And he really missed him. He missed him so much.

I had him cremated. I've got my little box with CJ, and my big box with Patrick. I want to scatter them together, one day, but it's been such a long time now. The longer I wait, the harder this becomes.

PAUL B

Paul emerges from his nightmarish state with some medical help and finds hope in the company of strangers.

I think after Leanne died I was very keenly aware of this apocalyptic grief, and then after the medication, about six weeks later, I remember standing in the kitchen and thinking, "Oh my god. I am free!" So there was a sense of like, for the first time, I was not having that continual shock or that anxiety about where am I going to be tomorrow, what state am I going to be in, is this going to be for eternity? In other words, for a moment I got a breather, and I stopped that awful flow of grief and was able to just sit down for a moment. For so long I felt like I was just getting banged around, getting hit with memory after memory rolling about, of her hair falling out, her vomiting, her falling down, and me helping her back up in the hallway, and getting her to the toilet, and getting her neck brace on for the night, and her bedding routine.

And then watching her go.

So the medication afforded me what seemed like a minute's breather from what had been this internal holocaust. It was good to stop shaking and shuddering and wondering whether or not I was actually going to make it.

Then that weekend I summoned the courage to go out. It was a year and a half since I had been out. Of all things, I went to a singles' house party. It seemed the total antithesis to the place that I had been in. I had been locked away doing the house and the kids for so long I found I was getting a bit of 'cabin fever'. I hadn't been out in the world, communicating with others, and I needed to be with adults. It was an acknowledgement that, "Yes, I am entitled to a life after all." It was odd, very odd, but it was also good. For the first time in a long time, I was able to function away from the house and with a crowd. I had been able to get clear, and stand alone in a room and chat to some people. I walked around, chatted with a couple of guests, met the host, and had a great time. I actually met someone there, and under different circumstances it may have worked. It didn't.

I think statistically, men, more than women, will tend to go out and find another relationship to help them deal with their loss, and it's the worse thing you can do. But it's just learning: we fall and we learn and we get up.

So this was a first step. It was a first run.

It was pretty miraculous really.

6

An Awakening

Just as day follows night, and night follows day, the beating of our hearts slowly gains new vitality. Over time this emerging strength softens the fracturing that has gone before.

In the newfound safety of this steady beat, the first glimpses of happiness become apparent.

Healing is underway.

In tiny baby steps or giant leaps of faith, we move beyond the grip of darkness towards the freedom of light and new life.

Journal Entry

17th August 2004

The sun has just descended over the hills on the horizon setting
on this, the second anniversary of your death.

Today, I did not make the pilgrimage to the cemetery as I
had planned.

I have been getting run down, and today it has got the better
of me. Tomorrow I go to the doctor's perhaps?

But today, after another bad night's sleep, I chose not to make
the journey. Too tired!

I almost changed my mind when a re-run of *Mad About You* came
on the telly. Have been thinking a lot about that show lately for
some reason – and out of the blue, there it was!

It was one of our absolute favourite TV shows! We loved it so
much! That, and *Touched By An Angel*, and that one, *'Play With
Me Daddy'* – I can't remember what it was called, but the little
boy kept saying this to his dad – and *Twin Peaks* and *The X-Files*.
I remember when we were living in at Mum and Dad's, in that
tiny room, and either after tea or sometimes with a plate of food
each for dinner we would retreat into our hideaway and escape
into the fantasy world of these crazy TV shows.

Seeing *Mad About You* brought all that back. All those crazy,
inconsequential things we never gave a second thought to,
they were just part of the fabric of our life.

I feel that world fading.

I fear that world fading.

Somehow, perhaps and ever so subtly, over the last several months, my 'New Life' is taking hold. I am very, very slowly feeling as though I am in a life of my own. It has slowly become more solid. At first I felt so empty and one-dimensional: the warmth and constant glow that your presence had been in my life was now absent.

I can and do get sad, quite a lot, still, but a new feeling has emerged and I guess this is a kind of a healing? I don't know. It's not so much that I feel happy. I don't. I don't know if I ever will know what that sense of happiness feels like anymore. No, it's more a kind of 'solid'.

I cannot think of you though. For then this locked vault in which my other life 'lives' is opened, and the feelings overwhelm me and the sadness takes over.

So, sometimes, I deliberately choose not to think about you. Sometimes this is completely beyond my control, like a flashback hitting me, or I hear a certain song, or see someone that reminds me of you. Then, I have little control over my feelings. At other times, I very deliberately try to not think about you.

This is new.

But the loss has been so great, so far-reaching: the loss of a shared youth that was alive because you were; of the children we were to have, those little spirits destined to be born into our lives now robbed of their birth; of the many beautiful conversations and experiences and full and vibrant living we were to have shared; the reminiscences exchanged in our irreverently disgraceful old age; and all the many, many other things that were waiting for us to experience on our journey together.

I mourn the dissolution of this dream.
Our dream.
The dream we both once held for us.

But mostly I mourn the loss of You.
Of the familiar, beautiful, charismatic You.

And the impact of your death has also taken its toll on my family; it has been their loss too, of their son and brother-in-law, of the grandchildren, nieces, nephews and little cousins we would have given our family that they will now never know; and of the future implied by our union, a future of which we were all once a part, now changed.

Whilst life never promises any guarantees, it is the simple things that one treasures most – family, relationship, and the continuity of a life together – that one takes for granted and assumes above all else, will be sustained and strengthened by the passage of time, not ripped away and broken apart.

In the midst of change and unpredictability I always truly believed that we would be the constant; that in a world of change, our living bond would hold strong.

How naïve I have been. How terribly, terribly naïve! Now I know so much better.
Now I really know things.
About life. About change.
About fragility and impermanence.
And mostly, about Love.

Conversations

BEV

Appreciating life and focusing on the practicalities of the everyday have enabled Bev to be present to the possibilities of a future in which Peter no longer plays a role.

I think the lives of those who have not experienced death are a little bit poorer than the lives of those of us who have. Death makes you truly appreciate the people you have around you and also you are so aware that it can come knocking at any time. And so this prospect makes you very alert to expressing yourself openly, and taking care of the details, the little things; as the old proverb suggests, you must make sure that you live everyday as if it were your last.

This is not about doom and gloom; it's a positive, uplifting way to live. Because if I were to die tomorrow, while it would be sad because I wouldn't get to see my kids and my grandkids and all that sort of thing, I would know that I couldn't have done any more in my life if I'd tried, and that I hadn't left a mess for everybody else to take care of. I've committed myself to making the world a better place than how I found it, so I'd go away from it feeling, "Yes, this is okay."

So death can shape the rest of your life in a most powerful and fantastic way.

What helps me now is the knowledge that I must work to resolve everything so I can move on into the future. This has meant dealing with all the legalities, all the financials, all the concrete stuff, and until that's all resolved, that is my purpose. And anyway, it's very difficult to move on when you've got to deal with those things. You can't actually start a new life. At my age, I didn't anticipate starting a new career, but I have to; I have to totally remake my whole life. I ran Peter's businesses, I ran the Foundation, and we were still joint directors of companies, so suddenly, with his death, everything is completely different. So for me now, until everything is resolved, it's very difficult to wipe the slate clean and say, "Okay, this is a new chapter of my life." I'm really still in a transition phase.

The thing I find now is that with a lot of the public speaking I do, people will focus on the fact that I was Peter's partner for so long, and so because I've always worked with life skills, stress management and personal development, I have had to find a way to get those same messages through but in relating it to our life's journey.

There's a museum being set up in his honour, and I am working with the people who are setting up the museum. There are still many facets that have yet to be put in place that in many respects shouldn't involve me but do because I was the only one who was really there for the entire time, the only one who has the complete history. But I can see that coming to an end soon and the kids being able to take over. And that'll be good because I don't want to have a front role in any of this. I just want to be able to hand it over and for the kids to keep their father's memory going. It's not my place to do that. I'm looking forward to that time when I can completely step back from all this and just be my own person, and hopefully create a new life.

Peter and I were both people who didn't have dreams or goals as such, we were in the moment, and we made the most of the moment. He trusted in the way the future was going to unfold. And I don't for a moment sit and think about what my future's going to be, I just know that if I devote myself totally one hundred percent to whatever I'm doing, and embrace whatever opportunities come along, it's going to evolve.

And if there's something positive that can come out of my experience, then I'll use it to help other people.

KERRI

Although she mourns the loss of the hopes and dreams she and Jeff once held, Kerri finds much on which to place great value.

I went away last month for my first girls' weekend with my tennis team. It was for one night. I had to pack for four of us and each kid went somewhere different. Beforehand it just did not feel worth the effort, but it turned out to be very relaxing while I was there. But as soon as I returned and picked up one child, met the other, and then a friend to take them horse riding, then drove that friend home and then finally picked up the last child, I felt as though the whole weekend away had been just a dream. Plus, I felt really guilty leaving the children, although I understand that this has more to do with my own issues which I need to deal with better, because in fact I know that the kids all had a great time and I'm sure the people who looked after them were happy to have them to stay.

I often think of people who are a lot worse off than I am; divorced women who have the constant torment of their ex-husband who doesn't care for his children and goes about flaunting his new life. But then I see that the kids at least still have their dad in their lives and ultimately the responsibility for the kids is shared.

I hate it when people suggest that life is getting easier now that three and a half years have passed, when it is actually getting harder because there are new and different challenges each day. There is nothing easy about losing your best friend, and losing all your hopes and dreams as a family, and then trying to gather the strength to create an entirely new future. I try not to think of the future, except that hopefully it will be easier and happier. I am just going through the motions of everyday life with this constant sadness and loneliness in the background.

It sounds like I am leading a miserable life, which I am not: I have great friends; we have been lucky to have had great holidays; I have a supportive family; my kids seem as though they are going really well at school and getting along well with their friends; and Claire is always happy.

It is just that it would have been so much better sharing all these things with Jeff.

LINDA

Linda's resilience is restored at its own pace.

Am I coping? Yes. Does my heart still bleed and hurt? Yes it does. Have I got on with my life? Yes I have. I have had to. I've got some good people around me, good support, and I'm just chugging along. When Rick got sick, and then after his death, it was one breath at a time, it was one minute, it was five minutes, it was ten minutes, an hour, it was half a day, it was a day. I think I'm at about the half-day measure, maybe at a day sometimes.

ROSE

Learning about suicide, and meeting others who have had similar experiences has given Rose the conviction and courage to start rebuilding her life.

Recovery is dealt with differently by different people, and grieving has its stages, but I'm a big believer in the fact that people will experience these stages of shock, disbelief, denial, anger, grief and acceptance differently, not all in the same order, and for different lengths of time. Honesty, self-honesty, is important in being able to acknowledge and recognise these feelings. It's a little like having to check your emails and read them: if they're not sorted out and are just ignored, eventually there's a great build-up of unread files and it just slows down the system. It just means having to clear out more, later.

Some friends or family in some way felt guilty about my husband's passing, and this can be a natural reaction and emotion with any person's passing, regardless of how they died. What I have learnt is that people cannot be held to blame for the actions of a suicidal person. It is never any one person or thing that is responsible, but a number of contributing factors that, sometimes even without our knowing, may already have been there. It is not what was said or left unsaid. It is not what was done or left undone. It is not any one person who is responsible for someone's decision to end his or her life. Blame will be aimed at many people, and usually those who attribute blame are in denial themselves. It is these people who can make life really tough.

It was my experience, unfortunately, to be the recipient of harsh and cruel accusations, to be blamed for the lack of commitment in preventing my husband's death. Blame also came from his side of the family. This was a tough one to deal with as my children, being as young as they were, were confused by these so-called friends' and family's alienation. Thankfully, there were some people who stood by us and with whom we still have contact today.

Early on in the aftermath, I was so angry with certain accusations that I wrote all that I was feeling in a notebook. I felt like I was going to burst if I didn't. I wrote all that I wanted to say as though I was saying it to all of them. Word by word. This was a kind of closure for me as far as they were all concerned. Writing can be so very healing.

I believe it is imperative that anyone affected by a person's suicide should speak with someone about it. This helped my children and me immensely. My priority was to see the children through the catastrophe as unscathed as possible, so I sought counselling of different kinds for us as a family: traditional, religious, and spiritual.

Talking about it as often as we needed to is what helped us, and not only us, friends also. Death, especially suicide, should never be taboo. People always seemed to have questions. They were confused because they thought he was happy. I found myself constantly explaining to give them some clarity.

I have met many people affected by suicide, and my experience has been that attitude is what makes the difference. Knowing that there is such a large community of people out there whose lives are impacted made me realise we were not alone. I learnt early on in life that, at least for me, there are only two ways of dealing with issues: I could do nothing, and remain absorbed with sadness and grief, becoming a victim in the process, or I could ask, "Okay, where to from here? What do I need to do now?"

The reality for me in all of this was that 'forward' was the only way to go, and I felt that I didn't need to wait to be ready to do so. I found that telling myself first and then doing so seemed to be a natural course of action for me to take and this has become a habit. I was not about to let my children's lives and my own life take a turn in the wrong direction! Our happiness relied on me, so taking care of my family and our happiness was exactly what I intended to do!

It won't always be, and it certainly has not been easy, and there will be reminders for us along the way, such as a person's resemblance to Andrew, someone's comment, a news article or story, a book or film. Even someone's name can trigger a host of emotions. These have become easier to deal with over time, and at times tend to fill a void, depending on how I look at it. For example, my daughter today was standing next to a tall man with his young child in the supermarket, and she thought how nice it felt, reminding her of her father and thinking for just a moment how it may have felt to have him standing next to her. In the early days, something like this would have made her sad. Perspective changes in time.

I believe that nothing stays the same. Children are extraordinarily resilient and we can learn a thing or two from them. One thing I learnt from my children through all of this was to embrace the child within me, because it never leaves us. It lies dormant within our minds and hearts; we just need to learn to recognise triggers that remind us to retrieve a childlike perspective once in a while. It can be a humbling experience.

Life is not perfect for us, but we are happy. Besides, he would be happier knowing that we are. All good things that come along the way are just a bonus.

JUNE

June now believes that professional grief counselling early on might have helped her cope better with her loss. However these days, simple pleasures such as a cup of tea and putting her feet up take on fresh meaning.

I think in many ways I was silly because I tried to do it all on my own. I thought, "I can deal with this!" whereas perhaps I should have got some help. And I think that stems from when I came out to Australia, not having my mum here, having to cope on my own. It's like when you're sick, you always want your mum, don't you? And I needed my mum when this happened, but she'd passed away anyway, and she would have been in England so it wouldn't have been any good after all. So I felt I had to deal with it on my own.

I don't think it was such a good idea now. There is help out there. If I had gone and spoken to a counsellor, they might have told me, "Okay now you could feel this, you could feel that, and this could happen or that can happen and that's okay, that's normal, it's okay to feel like that." To get some help may have made a difference to how I was coping with everything.

People kept saying to me, "Are you angry?" and I kept telling them I wasn't which was true at first. I was very upset and sad for David that he wasn't around to see his grandchildren, and missing the beautiful sunny days in Warrandyte. We lived a very basic, sheltered life, there were no airs and graces, no money, but it was a happy life! And I kept thinking it was so sad he was missing all this! He should have been here sharing it with me.

I did get angry down the track. I suppose I was being selfish because I was thinking of myself, of what I had lost. I was angry and sad that we were not going to grow old together like I had planned, and have the little English cottage garden, and live in that little cottage, with me baking cakes and the smell of fresh bread coming out of the house and him out in the garden or pottering around in his shed. Living a long life, and growing old together. That was my plan, that was my dream, and that dream was shattered beyond belief.

It is seven years ago that David died. So it's taken me seven years to be able to start getting back on track to how I was before. But I am a different person. You have to change. How can your life not change?

You know, David's in my pot out there. Same with Nod, our dog. We've taken half of his ashes to Philip Island, and half of it's got to go back to the UK because that's what he wanted done. So we'll do that.

He was in a little box there on my hearth. That's how we picked him up from the crematorium. I used to have him by my side here, and put my cup of tea on him, or I'd put my feet on him and use him as my footrest!

And when Nod passed away, I got a beautiful timber box with her name on it. I looked at David's crumpled down cardboard box (I mean, he was in a container, inside the box!) and I thought, "Oh, you look a bit pathetic in that, don't you mate? We'll get you something nice!" And so he's in a nice blue and white ceramic pot. But he is always here. And Nod's always here. I haven't sprinkled Nod around yet; I mean, I will do that eventually.

I'm not ready to take David to England yet. It's different. I can go down the island and think, "Oh yeah, I sprinkled some there." Paul and Jody both came with me and we all had a little bag each, and we all sprinkled him everywhere. So he's all over the island. But to go back to the UK and sprinkle him there like he wanted, I'm not ready to do that yet, to let the rest of him go, not yet.

Perhaps one day.

Listening to other people's stories in a bereavement support group provides Elwyn with a different perspective on his own experience. He accepts now, that Cathy has truly gone.

At times when I feel sad, I pick up one of the photos of Cathy and talk to her. I tell her how much I love her and how proud she must be of the way the kids have turned out. I tell her that she will always remain young and beautiful.

Cathy's favourite song was *Endless Love*. I taped it for her and played it in the car when we left our wedding reception. Every time I hear that song I listen intently to every single word and think of her.

I like the way some of Cathy's mannerisms have surfaced, especially with my girls. If they want something, they tilt their head slightly and flick their eyelashes and say, "Please Dad." Whenever Cathy did that she always got what she wanted!

I found the support group for Younger Bereaved Partners to be an enormous help to me, especially early on in my grief. Knowing I was not alone in that situation made a big difference. I finally found people who could relate to my feelings. I had previously lost both my parents, however it did not compare with the loss I felt when Cathy passed away.

Listening to some of their stories was so heartbreaking, as I knew exactly what they were going through. Some had the added stress of court cases with wills being contested and custody battles with grandparents, financial pressures from the loss of a job, no support from family or friends and so on.

Suddenly my situation didn't seem so bad after all, and in a strange way that made me feel a bit better.

What has helped me find peace is accepting the fact that Cathy is really gone and that I can't change history. I have to deal with the present situation as well as I can, while still staying focused on my kids' best interests. I find it comforting to think that Cathy would be proud of me for the way the kids are today. It brings me great joy to hear the sound of the three of them laughing together when they hear something funny.

I feel emotionally stronger now and don't have any need for a special place to be alone. Time has made people less aware of my situation, and I don't seem to have the label of widower anymore.

At first I could not imagine ever moving on and letting go. As time went by, about eighteen months, I gradually got used to being without Cathy, and I would wake up in the morning no longer expecting her to be lying next to me. A new 'normal' life had emerged, although I still have the memories, which I doubt will ever fade.

Some of Cathy's clothes which have sentimental value still hang in my wardrobe. Her rings have gone to my two daughters, and we have her photos displayed around the house. I also have Cathy's ashes on a table next to my bed. She always considered our bed to be especially comfortable, and on occasions I put her ashes on her side of the bed next to me when I go to bed.

I started attending a 'Further down the Track' group at Younger Bereaved Partners where new relationships were discussed. I was generally happy with my life: I still enjoy my job, I have a large circle of friends, a loving family, good health, and play tennis regularly. All this sounds really good, but at the end of the day I was missing that special person to share the rest of my life with. I came to the conclusion that single life is not so great, and that I did want to eventually find another partner.

One person in the bereavement group talked about meeting people on the Internet, and I had a work colleague who was also doing the same. I decided to give it a try and soon found myself talking to a few people. My children were pleased for me, and I eventually went out with a lady, but that didn't work out. A few months later I met someone else who proposed to me after five months. A month after we were engaged, I realised she may have been marrying me for the wrong reasons, and we split up. I'm hoping I will one day find that special person to grow old gracefully with.

PAUL S

Paul finds comfort knowing that Delina's pain has ended.

Knowing that Delina is no longer suffering brings some relief. It really broke my heart to see her suffering so much, and knowing that there was nothing on Earth that I could do for her.

Sometimes, I find solace in listening to the music that Delina liked. I close my eyes and picture better times of our life together, and Delina dancing to the music.

There is comfort in knowing that one day I will be with her again.

One day I will be with my beautiful Delina again.

Laughter's return heralds the possibility that Erika will experience joy once again.

They say that the loss never really stops hurting, that the sadness stays with you, always. But my sadness has changed in the last three years, has got less. In its place there is a growing feeling of gratefulness for having had what we had. Gratefulness to have met someone that was as perfect for me as Damian was. The loss is there, still, but it is gradually filled with the wonder at how lucky I was to have found Damian in the first place – and the realisation that something in his love has outlived him, is around still, unbeatable, supporting me in every step I have taken since the day he died.

This third year has been about building. Building onto the house; building up a new CD collection, because I cannot listen to any music from our previous lives; and building towards a new career that he had always encouraged me to take up.

At some point, during this third year, a little flame appeared at the end of the tunnel. A tickle in my throat, announcing laughter had returned, some hope for future happiness – some prospect of a life that could be strong and joyful again. I can feel this flame popping up, more and more often. It came with the successes in building, and with seeing myself increasingly as an independent person again, someone who chooses to maintain strong bonds with in-laws and friends, rather than as a victim of a cruel fate who needs them for support. There is little I have come to hate as much as having to ask for support, and needing the support of others, mainly in terms of help with looking after the kids. And I have developed a monumental appreciation for those people who have the ability to offer their help without it appearing like a favour. It can be such a drag, asking for sleepovers for your kids, and I love them for their effort in convincing me that it is in fact me who is doing them a favour.

One day, when the kids grow older and we might no longer live so close, these relationships will be entirely reliant on the love and friendship we are building now.

My boys' life would be so different with Damian around. He was the competent parent; I am the struggler who just manages. I am not made of the material that single parents need to be made of. I was so confidant that the boys would of course grow up to be great men, because they had a dad who was. Someone said that I need to stop trying to be both mum and dad for them, and just be mum. But what if mum isn't great at being mum? I try, sometimes succeeding, sometimes not.

And I need to take medical precautions for them. I became obsessed with finding the answer to the causes of Damian's sudden death. I became an expert in the latest research on coronary artery disease, the link with stress, and with cardiac arrhythmias. In an online-community for young widowed parents I had posted a question about medical check-ups for the children, and found that most people had taken this very seriously, so I went back to the paediatrician and asked for a referral to a paediatric cardiologist. Now we have a plan in place for regular check-ups over the next years. I can sleep more easily with that.

The boys and I have never stopped talking about Damian. Their grandma and aunty made a book of stories and pictures about Damian as a boy, which we read together. We look at the pictures and tell stories of him. I want them to feel as proud of their dad as other kids are of their dads.

They know about the spirit of the dead. I took the idea to them, but they have a better understanding of it than I do. My older son looked at the sun rising up behind a bit of bushland early one morning, a month after Damian had died. The rays of the sun were clearly visible, shining through between the trees. He told me then that the rays of the sun are like the spirit of the dead. They follow you wherever you go.

At the beginning of Year One at school my son told his class that his dad had died. The teacher handled it well, and I was so sad and yet so happy that he could deal with this type of situation. I think it's partly because we started meeting up with the kids of my support group. Seven kids who lost dads and three who lost their mothers. We are not trained; we just do our own thing. The kids use our get-togethers as a space to talk about their dads. They make things that tell a story of their dad and of their lives with him and after. The kids love going, and are proud to be part of this group. I think that is why my son had the inner strength to talk about Damian in class.

Now, just before the third anniversary of losing Damian, it sometimes still hits me like an unbelievable nightmare, that it just could not have happened, surely not to me. There is an image that lingers, of the other life, the one we should have had. But then my life takes new turns every day, and that image of what our life together could have been becomes more distant and a bit unreal.

In its stead, a new reality is unfolding. Maybe there will be love again, at some point. I would like that to happen. I am no good alone, and Damian knows that. He is with me, never limiting or constraining, always supporting me, opening up opportunities, believing in me, believing that I will make the right choices for myself and the boys, even if I get it wrong here and there along the way.

That is his eternal gift to me.

ANN

A gift for Patrick helps Ann honour his spirit, and in time she begins to accept life as it now is.

The night before Patrick had the heart attack, I had decided to start quilting, and I got a book with a whole lot of pictures of all sorts of quilts, not quilt patterns, just quilts, and I picked out six and asked him which one he would like. And he chose one of them, it was very structured, with quite a structured design, and he said, "I really need structure in my life at the moment."

And then he had his heart attack the next day.

After he died, I decided to do a beginners' patchwork class, just to get some basic techniques before I started to do a quilt, and I had an idea that I would like to do a memory quilt for Patrick but I didn't know what; there were a few ideas, one where he had wanted to design a Japanese garden so I thought of making a quilt with that design in it. But in the end, I didn't have the time or the headspace to design it. So a design that came up one day in the quilting shop where I was doing the class was a mariners' compass quilt, a specific design, which has got a compass pattern on it. I thought it would be perfect for Patrick because he loved the water, he loved sailing, and he loved old wooden things and all of that old mariners' stuff. And then I came across this fabric one day and it was perfect for the background for the compass, and then I based the other fabrics around the idea of its being midnight, on a wooden boat, way out at sea, and with a background that is very, very dark. The other colours are very muted, so the quilt expresses the notion of dark seas and dark night, with a compass pointing north for the directional reference, with his colours, and the idea of it being a very quiet, peaceful midnight, on this boat. Because I don't actually do the quilting, I just construct the quilt top, and send it to a woman who does machine quilting. I told her the whole story, and she designed the quilt around these themes. She understood the concept completely, and did a fabulous job quilting.

So that's how the quilt came about. I love that quilt. I didn't end up doing a formal memory quilt, which isn't really my thing anyway when I think about it, but this quilt had stuff related to it that made sense. Doing the quilt has been very therapeutic.

One thing I found frustrating about all that suffering and all that pain is that it didn't make me any more capable of dealing with all the interpersonal stuff with the living! All the stuff like, "I know that you can just drop dead tomorrow, so I don't worry about all that trivial stuff any more!" It happened in bits and pieces, and in the short term, but it's amazing how quickly life reverted back to the trivial and the little slights at work or tiffs here or resentment there. Perhaps it doesn't happen as much as it did before, but there have been many times when I have felt as uncomfortable and self-conscious as I once did, so this life-changing situation didn't work for me much in that sense. I'm sure it has changed me in lots of ways that are more positive, but I'm aware of the fact that I can still get caught up in the trivial, the mediocre and the inconsequential.

I suppose one of the biggest adjustments was going back to the whole 'single and alone' thing. Prior to Patrick, I had been just that for such a long time that it was normal for me, and there was the whole question of whether I was going to find anyone and whether I'd ever have a partner and then finally I did at thirty-six, nearly thirty-seven, and then six years later he was dead.

It took me so long to find him, and then he was gone so soon. Who else could believe in me like Patrick? Who else could ask for a hug the way he did? Who else has the extraordinary combination of gentleness, strength, danger and compassion?

For a long time I didn't see myself as single, and I still don't like that term particularly, it sort of implies things; but I certainly don't refer to myself as married either. For the first twelve months after he had died I was married as far as I was concerned. I guess what has been different is I used to have this notion that, "Oh well, I'll re-partner then!" Not straight away, but I was kind of hoping I would in about three years, because I thought that being on my own again for three years was about as long as I could deal with, having decided that being partnered was quite nice. Three years was also about the length of the doctoral study and that was meant to be a period of suffering! Yeah, so I thought I'll do the three years of suffering, but then it would be really nice to re-partner in about three years, maybe four at a push? Yeah, sure!

I suppose when I finally moved out of that place, and completed my Doctorate, life slowly started to be about acceptance. This is my life. It's my dogs and me and now the cat, too. And I don't focus on what's missing in terms of a partner anymore; I think a partner would be nice, but I don't plan around it and focus on it now. Planning is the wrong word, but I suppose I used to think in terms of, "Well, hopefully by then I would have met someone, and I wouldn't have to do whatever." Or I'd think, "By the time I have to move out of the flat I would have met someone, and I'd be able to move out with someone, and by the time I've done such and such, then…" It was always a reference.

I think that this has been perhaps the biggest shift for me, finally acknowledging that this is my life; there's an acceptance that this is how things are. Things may not always be like this, but this is how they are for me at present and for the moment I am okay with this.

Paul's journey has revealed to him new ways of understanding the world.

Life without Leanne is the 'road not taken'. We all assume that we have as much time as we need to say it all and do it all with those we love. I think perhaps we need this belief and for it to be unquestionable in our minds. The reality is, of course, we may not have that time.

I ventured out into my new world somewhat like a toddler would, taking faltering steps towards a new horizon. Who was I? Where was I going? What was to become of me? How would I endure the despair? Would I be given some small understanding? Anything would do! I needed basic reassurances: I wasn't mad or going mad from grief, I was simply loaded to beyond my capacity and my reactions in this state were fair and reasonable.

Happiness has been elusive. And it hasn't been happiness so much as calm. I can't draw a line on the ground and say that's when I stepped over. I suppose the happiness is still emerging. I'm still walking towards collecting myself, reassessing, plus I'm approaching fifty, so that's a bit of a milestone; you're supposed to try and integrate all of these things. In some ways I'm a lot smarter now, and that's probably because I've learnt and read and studied; I'm a lot more aware of the ways of the world, and how relationships work, but I don't know whether it means I'm prepared to take the leap again.

I met her at twenty-six and I just fell, I gave her my heart, I gave her my all. Now at almost fifty, I'm not going to turn around and do that again, in the sense that it will be qualitatively different. I'm not projecting the same sorts of stuff because I've grown wiser I suppose, which is a good thing. It would be nice to be in love again, although I don't know if I should do that again because it can have all sorts of complications. But what I do know is that I have four kids for whom I am responsible. The challenge for me is to go out into the world creatively and professionally again.

After losing Leanne and after going into hospital myself and coming out, I looked around and it struck me: we all think that we are so different, yet look at how we rejoice and how we grieve. The great levellers: a birth and a death. We think we're so different, but just take a look around. Those monumental times when we are levelled, and all the rest in between when there is loving and celebrations and giving, it just opened my heart. That month after she passed, part of my survival was just allowing the community to nurture me, and the gratitude for that carried me, and I thought, "Is not everyone entitled to the same?" The guy who has fallen, he's just another brother; and I was definitely one of the fallen. I was blessed or lucky or whatever to have that community to come along and just scoop me up in those arms of support, you know. And that was just a miracle really.

There has been a gratitude for having Leanne, for the children, to have been able to have that love. But there was also deep rage and absolute horror and contempt at the injustice, and railing against the higher power, I suppose. Harold Kushner wrote in his book, *When Bad Things Happen to Good People*, that God cannot control every single event, movement, or second and that we are free to choose how we will use our free will. The consequences will be either uplifting or devastating. Ultimately bad things can and do happen in the world, irrespective of whatever gifts that may or may not come along years later, but I think one has to be human, and it is human to wrestle, to struggle and to fall. To lose Leanne was a tremendous loss, but I am the adult so I have to try and sift what good there may be out of it. My children, on the other hand, have lost their mother; they won't have what they've wanted, what they crave. They don't have her arms to hold them, they don't have what I used to love to see, her reading to our little ones, and for them to have from their mum the confirmation of their worth as human beings and her always there to help, you know? That's shit – pardon the language; that's injustice. I wonder what it will be like for them later in life; to say I lost my mother when I was seven, eight, or thirteen?

Kahil Gilbran, in *The Prophet*, says, "Your joy is your sorrow unmasked. And the selfsame well from which your laughter rises was oftentimes filled with your tears." It breaks open your heart, but does it keep our heart open, does it keep us loving? If we had no adversity, would we just be stone? Perhaps yes, perhaps no, who can say. I've been looking for the gold out of this and I haven't found the answer, but I have little clues along the way because I went looking. Some people just take their rage out on the world and go and shoot people.

How we respond to what happens in our lives is deeply subjective; each person has their own needs and methods and ways of seeing. I was lucky enough to be supported; I was also given time to go looking, so the universe has been more than generous, in that sense, for which I am deeply grateful.

I went out there and learnt, and studied, and read, and talked to people, and joined groups. Sometimes I get tired and fall down and have crap days and judge my fellow man and get worried about climate change and water resources and all of that, but I have changed as a person.

In many ways, my children saved me. I care for them and am responsible for them and became deeply involved with their interior life, and always made myself available to them. I also knew that they were her. Really, they were her; so I kept close to them and I keep close to her.

That was my salvation.

It has been almost eight years and my recovery has been an arduous uphill climb, with many a wonderful person walking with me on that narrow trail. Emotionally, and in every other way, I owe my recovery to my children, to the support of my community and to my medications.

Without this help, God knows where I would be now.

7

After You

Life without Stu

A Photograph

There is a photograph.
In it two strangers:
A handsome young man
His life ending tragically
Too few years from when the photo is taken;
The young woman, her life soon buffeted
By winds of fate, challenge, and adversity.
There is something familiar about this photo
Yet at the same time something unfamiliar.
It is as if I know them
But I know that I cannot possibly
Know these people any longer.
These people are like strangers.
What I do know now
Is how once upon a time
The stars conspired for these strangers to meet
Destiny weaving theirs paths into one
Entwined years of possibility
Now mapped out before them
Two Souls in a dance
Of laughter and tears,
Of hopes and of fears
But all ending too soon
It had barely begun
And he left without saying goodbye.

Journal Entry

January 26th 2006

I am on a bus.

Outside, the land is parched, trees and grass are brown, the weather hot.

Inside, it is cool.

It is quiet.

The sound of soft murmuring wafts its way in and out of my awareness. I am one of two women in a crowd of about fifty weary blokes, gladly heading back from the mountains towards home.

I press my face to the window and feel the coolness of the glass against my skin. This big open space we silently roll through, the vast expanse of darkening blue skies and pale fluffy clouds yet not a drop of rain in sight, suddenly remind me of you. We loved big skies and this beautiful, rugged continent that was our home; that is my home.

The familiar sting of silent tears catches me by surprise. In this vastness, I am vulnerable still. All around me are people who know nothing of the person I used to be. I keep her secreted away, concealed behind a cheerful disposition and cheeky grin. I blink away the tears before this other me is seen.

Being miles from home and hanging out with a bunch of strangers collectively engaged in efforts to halt the ravages of bushfire, gives me the freedom of anonymity and the focus of pure purpose; it allows me to blend into something far bigger than myself, bringing me swiftly and absolutely into the present. This new 'real' facilitates a safe distance between the pain of losing what was and the reality of what now is.

And yet.

And yet, just when I think I am okay, just when I think I am safe, a look, a smile, a song, a place, and the sadness of you no longer being alive taps me on my shoulder and quietly insists on its rightful place in my life.

So this is my truth now.
I am changed.
And yet, in some ways I am the same.
Through my tears and through our love, I have grown stronger.
This is who I am.
I am here
But I am also partly there,
Because you are always somewhere there,
Or here
With me.

Eulogy at Stu's Funeral, August, 2002

That we must love one another
Because life is short
That we must cherish our days
Because these are all we have
That it is never wrong, weak or shameful to ask
for help;
And that if someone does, we must give to them a
shoulder or open heart and be with them, for them, in
their struggle.
And that we must tell people how much we care about
them, setting aside all differences and prejudice,
Because the day will come when we no longer can,
and if we have not done so, then we will never again
be able to.
Please take Stu's lessons into your hearts.
Remember the soul that he was; cherish the memories
you have of him, and recall in times of doubt, the
lesson his life and death has taught us.